New Perspectives for Student Affairs Professionals:
Evolving Realities, Responsibilities and

by Peter H. Garland and Thomas W. Grace

ASHE-ERIC Higher Education Report No. 7, 1993

Prepared by

Clearinghouse on Higher Education
The George Washington University

In cooperation with

Association for the Study
of Higher Education

Published by

School of Education and Human Development
The George Washington University

Jonathan D. Fife, Series Editor

Cite as

Garland, Peter H., and Thomas W. Grace. 1993. *New Perspectives for Student Affairs Professionals: Evolving Realities, Responsibilities and Roles.* ASHE-ERIC Higher Education Report No. 7. Washington, D.C.: The George Washington University, School of Education and Human Development.

Library of Congress Catalog Card Number 94-66015
ISSN 0884-0040
ISBN 1-878380-28-1

Managing Editor: Bryan Hollister
Manuscript Editor: Barbara Fishel, Editech
Cover design by Michael David Brown, Rockville, Maryland

 # 30677679

The ERIC Clearinghouse on Higher Education invites individuals to submit proposals for writing monographs for the *ASHE-ERIC Higher Education Report* series. Proposals must include:
1. A detailed manuscript proposal of not more than five pages.
2. A chapter-by-chapter outline.
3. A 75-word summary to be used by several review committees for the initial screening and rating of each proposal.
4. A vita and a writing sample.

ERIC **Clearinghouse on Higher Education**
School of Education and Human Development
The George Washington University
One Dupont Circle, Suite 630
Washington, DC 20036-1183

This publication was prepared partially with funding from the Office of Educational Research and Improvement, U.S. Department of Education, under contract no. ED RR-93-0200. The opinions expressed in this report do not necessarily reflect the positions or policies of OERI or the Department.

EXECUTIVE SUMMARY

Colleges and universities today are confronted with a variety of changing conditions that demand attention; indeed, the formulation of appropriate and effective responses to a changing world has become increasingly important to institutions' vitality and viability. Changes in society, in the higher education enterprise, and in the types and characteristics of students are among those issues that must be addressed.

Increasingly, the efforts of student affairs aimed at improving student life, integrating new student groups, and attracting and retaining students are becoming critical to institutions attempting to maintain enrollments of qualified students, ensure academic achievement, place graduates, and develop supportive alumni. Institutions' use of these strategies in response to changing conditions creates opportunities for student affairs professionals to become leaders within institutions as they contribute significantly to institutions' viability. Under pressure to pare budgets, student affairs organizations must move quickly to demonstrate their centrality to institutional vitality or face disproportionate cuts in programs and services (Cage 1992).

To What Changes Must Student Affairs Organizations Respond?
Institutions and their student affairs organizations are confronted with various changes in their contexts and clienteles. The first of these trends, leading to change in society, is evidenced in uneven success with students from underrepresented groups in the education pipeline, demographic shifts, expanding use of information technologies, increasing violence, and the burden of debt. Second, institutions and their student affairs organizations must respond to the new accountability in higher education, even as public confidence in its colleges and universities erodes and new revenues become increasingly scarce. Colleges and universities find themselves subject to a growing array of state and federal statutes, regulations, initiatives, and judicial interventions.

In What Ways Can Student Affairs Offer Leadership To Respond to Changing Conditions?
In response to changing conditions, institutions are redoubling efforts to manage student enrollments—seeking new student clienteles while striving to retain students to graduation, employing quality management, modifying programs

and services to meet students' changing needs, seeking new sources of revenues while searching to contain costs, building partnerships, and focusing efforts to enhance students' involvement on campus.

Current efforts on campus suggest increasing congruity between the traditional goals of student affairs and broader institutional goals; research on efforts by student affairs organizations aimed at student development, once regarded as peripheral, demonstrates increasing importance to an institution's vitality (Astin 1992; Pascarella and Terenzini 1991). Student affairs organizations enhance students' involvement, working to establish multicultural environments, confronting violence on campus, managing enrollments, and helping faculty to understand students unlike themselves. As recognition grows for student affairs professionals' efforts in pursuit of the traditional goals of student development, an expanded role for student affairs is demanded.

What New Role Is Emerging for Student Affairs?
The student affairs organization shares the orientations of faculty, students, and administrators, and its position on the borders of these groups could be its greatest strength:

> *Truly, student personnel workers have the opportunities to be central figures for campus improvement in an era when resources must be perceived as newly combined rather than as new* (Silverman 1980, p. 12).

Further:

> *If the developmental model emerged in part to supply a positive and less reactive approach to student life, then we must now move to the next step to incorporate a positive approach to institutional life and to respond positively to the issues facing our institutions* (Smith 1982, p. 57).

Failing to accept this challenge could prove costly to the profession:

> *Student personnel work in the next 50 years will be called upon to perform even more significant functions than it has for the past 50. If it responds with creativity, ingenuity, and flexibility, there is no doubt of its future. If, however,*

it becomes the agent of the status quo and mere tradition,
other fields will assume its work, and it will be reduced to
performing mere housekeeping functions (Shaffer 1993,
p. 167).

In accepting this challenge, student affairs professionals can
become institutional integrators, creatively and collaboratively
integrating students' and the institution's development.

Serving as integrators within institutions, student affairs
professionals stand to become more centrally and integrally
involved in the direction of the institution. They will do so,
however, only if they are able to integrate and apply theories
of student development and institutional development, work
collaboratively with faculty and other administrators in developing comprehensive responses, and join with students in
recognizing the increasing need to integrate institutional practices with societal challenges and opportunities.

What Implications Does This New Role Have
For Student Affairs?

A new role for student affairs calls for changes in the programs
and services offered by student affairs, the professional skills
employed by student affairs professionals, and the content
of the preparation and continuing development of professionals. Several programs and services stand to be enhanced
by the changing role: enrollment management, the development of multicultural environments, and efforts to foster
community service, activism, and service learning.

To assume a more central position of leadership in the institution, student affairs professionals must possess a wider
repertoire of skills. Traditional skills required in the promotion of student development must be matched with the skills
needed to help the student affairs professional serve as environmental scanner, milieu manager, market analyst, legal
adviser, development officer, researcher, and quality assurance
specialist. In short, student affairs professionals must continue
to build their repertoire of skills to enable them to lead an
institution's efforts to develop comprehensive responses to
changing conditions.

The development of new skills for student affairs professionals has clear implications for the preparation and continuing professional development of individuals in the profession. Efforts to establish common learning for student

affairs professionals are still young (Hunter and Comey 1991) but hold great promise for defining the profession and its practice. Preparation programs tend to focus on administration or counseling, while emerging roles for student affairs professionals call for professionals who are competent in both counseling and administration and are able to integrate the skills of each to serve students and their institutions. As a result, graduate preparation programs must incorporate such studies as organizational development, quality management, planning, evaluation and research, and current issues in higher education. Further, continuing professional education must work toward the development and enhancement of professional knowledge and skills for new roles.

A new role also creates challenges for the application of student development. If student development is to offer guidance to the profession and become more useful to the student affairs integrator, then (1) the understanding and application of student development must become more integrated with practice in student affairs, (2) student development theory must encompass an increasingly diverse student population, and (3) student development and organizational development must become better integrated.

To better serve as integrators within the institution, student affairs professionals must:

1. Assess and understand the institutional environment;
2. Foster collaborative problem solving;
3. Develop professional collaboration with faculty;
4. Disseminate strategic information on students, their expectations, needs, interests, and abilities;
5. Translate goals for student affairs to others in the institution in meaningful terms;
6. Contribute to the quality of the academic experience;
7. Contribute to the effective and efficient management of the institution; and
8. Develop skills for a broader role.

Institutions, if they are to take advantage of current and future contributions of student affairs professionals should:

1. Recognize, enhance, and support the efforts of student affairs;

2. Consider student affairs professionals full partners in the institution; and
3. Challenge student affairs professionals to make greater contributions to the institution.

In addition, student personnel preparation programs must be reconceptualized to develop the broader skills necessary for the profession, including greater attention to skills of leadership, such as planning, management, and evaluation. And finally, associations of student affairs professionals must:

1. Continue to provide direction for a changing profession; and
2. Provide and promote continuing professional education at all levels.

ADVISORY BOARD

Barbara E. Brittingham
University of Rhode Island

Jay L. Chronister
University of Virginia

Rodolfo Z. Garcia
Michigan State University

Elizabeth M. Hawthorne
University of Toledo

Bruce Anthony Jones
University of Pittsburgh

L. Jackson Newell
University of Utah

Carolyn Thompson
State University of New York–Buffalo

CONSULTING EDITORS

Kimberly Brown
Portland State University

J. Kent Caruthers
MGT of America, Inc.

Elsa Kircher Cole
The University of Michigan

Jane F. Earley
Mankato State University

Walter H. Gmelch
Washington State University

James O. Hammons
University of Arkansas

Robert M. Hendrickson
The Pennsylvania State University

Barbara A. Lee
Rutgers University

Yvonna S. Lincoln
Texas A&M University

Robert J. Menges
Northwestern University

Kathleen Manning
The University of Vermont

Leila Moore
The Pennsylvania State University

Amaury Nora
University of Illinois–Chicago

Robert M. O'Neil
University of Virginia

Raymond V. Padilla
Arizona State University

Barbara S. Plakens
Iowa State University

Scott Rickard
Association of College Unions–International

William Rittenberg
Michigan State University

G. Jeremiah Ryan
Harford Community College

Kala Stroop
Southeast Missouri State University

John M. Swales
The University of Michigan

Ellen Switkes
University of California–Oakland

Jo Taylor
Wayne State University

Carolyn J. Thompson
State University of New York–Buffalo

Caroline Turner
University of Minnesota–Twin Cities

Elizabeth A. Williams
University of Massachuetts–Amherst

Richard A. Yanikoski
DePaul University

REVIEW PANEL

Charles Adams
University of Massachusetts–Amherst

Louis Albert
American Association for Higher Education

Richard Alfred
University of Michigan

Philip G. Altbach
State University of New York–Buffalo

Marilyn J. Amey
University of Kansas

Louis C. Attinasi, Jr.
University of Houston

Robert J. Barak
Iowa State Board of Regents

Alan Bayer
Virginia Polytechnic Institute and State University

John P. Bean
Indiana University

John M. Braxton
Vanderbilt University

Peter McE. Buchanan
Council for Advancement and
    Support of Education

John A. Centra
Syracuse University

Arthur W. Chickering
George Mason University

Shirley M. Clark
Oregon State System of Higher Education

Darrel A. Clowes
Virginia Polytechnic Institute and State University

John W. Creswell
University of Nebraska–Lincoln

Deborah DiCroce
Piedmont Virginia Community College

Richard Duran
University of California

Kenneth C. Green
University of Southern California

Edward R. Hines
Illinois State University

Marsha W. Krotseng
West Virginia State College and University Systems

George D. Kuh
Indiana University–Bloomington

Daniel T. Layzell
University of Wisconsin System

Meredith Ludwig
American Association of State Colleges and Universities

Mantha V. Mehallis
Florida Atlantic University

Robert J. Menges
Northwestern University

Toby Milton
Essex Community College

James R. Mingle
State Higher Education Executive Officers

Gary Rhoades
University of Arizona

G. Jeremiah Ryan
Harford Community College

Mary Ann Sagaria
Ohio State University

Daryl G. Smith
Claremont Graduate School

William Tierney
The Pennsylvania State University

Susan Twombly
University of Kansas

Harold Wechsler
University of Rochester

Michael J. Worth
The George Washington University

CONTENTS

FOREWORD

One of the first distinctive administrative positions in higher education, other than college president, was dean of students. It was created not out of a great concern for students' life outside the classroom but because the faculty felt that the combined role of teacher and disciplinarian was contradictory and dysfunctional. As the basic values of the German university model that promoted greater isolation of the faculty to pursue scholarship (freedom to teach) and greater independence among students (freedom to learn) were embraced for undergraduate education, it became more apparent that it was best to keep separate the intellectual nurturing role of the faculty from the negative role of disciplinarian so often associated with students' social life.

This separation had greater consequences than just administrative specialization, for it created a sense that students' nonclassroom or extracurricular experience was not a significant part of their education. Several reviews of the research on the impact of college on students disputed this concept, particularly *The Impact of Colleges on Students* (K.A. Feldman and T.M. Newcomb [San Francisco: Jossey-Bass, 1969]) and *How College Affects Students: Findings and Insights from Twenty Years of Research* (E. Pascarella and P.T. Terenzini [San Francisco: Jossey-Bass, 1991]). These researchers found that, after certain variables, such as natural maturation, are held constant, what distinct impact that be detected from the college experience can be attributed as much to experiences outside the classroom as to those in the classroom. And if one of the aims of colleges is to have a distinctive impact on their students, they need to integrate better total college experiences. Thus, higher education institutions could greatly increase their impact on students if they reversed the practice of separating the roles of student affairs administrators from those of faculty and began to develop a partnership that would create a more unified environment.

The role of student affairs or student life administrators as integrators has taken on an equally important function in the overall administration of an institution. As Peter H. Garland, assistant commissioner for postsecondary and higher education in the Pennsylvania Department of Education, and Thomas W. Grace, ombudsman for the Department of Housing and Residence Life and adjunct associate professor in higher education administration at New York University, discuss in *New Perspectives for Student Affairs Professionals:*

Evolving Realities, Responsibilities and Roles, the management of higher education institutions is seen increasingly as an interrelated, systematic process. Each administrative position and action has an impact on and is reacted to by some other part of the institution. The effect of the actions of student affairs administrators must be considered when developing an institution's strategic plan. For example, the successful accomplishment of academic goals is now seen as interdependent with the policies and procedures of the residence halls and the student center—places where students socialize and study. The quality of entering freshmen is determined by the effectiveness of the enrollment management office, which is influenced by the general satisfaction of the current student body and recent graduates. Both faculty and general administrators of a higher education institution are gradually seeing that, if they are to be successful, they must include student affairs in planning. In return, student affairs staff are realizing that they need to develop new skills if they are to integrate successfully with the organization's other cultures.

Organizations can no longer operate successfully without taking into consideration the interrelationship of each organizational unit. The research on the impact of college demonstrates the importance of the extracurricular for students' growth. The recent literature on management points to the wisdom of team efforts in developing goals and procedures. The role that student affairs can play as an integrator between the many units of an institution is enormous, but this role will not be achieved by accident. It will take new skills learned through continuous training and a new way of thinking about the interrelationship of student affairs with the mission of the institution. *New Perspectives for Student Affairs Professionals* will be very useful in stimulating the discussions to facilitate these changes.

Jonathan D. Fife
Series Editor, Professor of Higher Education Administration, and Director, ERIC Clearinghouse on Higher Education

ACKNOWLEDGMENTS

Many individuals contributed to bringing this work to fruition. We thank the many colleagues, students, and tolerant friends from whom we have learned and on whom we have tested the ideas presented in this report. Even before the ideas emerged for this project, certain individuals in each of our professional lives were essential in shaping our views and outlooks, including Leila Moore, Robert Hendrickson, and M. Lee Upcraft of Pennsylvania State University, Helga Orrick of Case Western Reserve University, and John Morgan of Maryville College in Missouri. We greatly appreciate our colleagues at the Pennsylvania Department of Education and New York University, who have been so supportive in general and, specifically, for the many hours this project has taken.

Jonathan Fife, series editor for the ASHE-ERIC Higher Education Reports, must be credited with the suggestion to return to the ideas presented in *Serving More Than Students,* test their currency, and explicate them for the 1990s.

Finally, we wish to thank our families, particularly our young children, whose patience will now be duly rewarded.

THE EVOLVING ROLE OF STUDENT AFFAIRS

Higher education in the United States is characterized by continuing evolution to meet the changing needs of society. Colonial colleges served society by preparing clergymen and societal leaders through a pious liberal arts curriculum for those few men who would become church and political leaders (Moore 1990; Rudolph 1962). During the next hundred years, an industrializing society needed a wider variety of social, political, and business leaders. Institutions of higher education responded by educating students for a wider range of roles in society and sought to serve society more directly through pure and applied research. After World War II, returning GIs and their children challenged educational institutions to provide education in an ever-widening array of careers and to open educational opportunity to all. New academic programs, new means of delivery, new types of students, and expanding roles for institutions in research, technological application, and continuing education have led to the colleges and universities of today.

Serving students well is being rediscovered as an essential and defining goal of institutions of higher education.

This ongoing evolution has not occurred without pain. More important, dynamic institutions in concert with an equally dynamic society have created exciting opportunities for those on and off campus. And like the institutions it is part of, student affairs has evolved over time.

In colonial colleges, the student affairs function, performed by faculty and tutors, was central to these institutions' goals for intellectual and moral development. With the growth of the extracurriculum and attempts to enliven the collegiate experience, expanding enrollments, and increasingly professional faculty, more diverse and complex institutions of the 19th century called for administrators to coordinate and advise a growing number of extracurricular programs and services (Rudolph 1962). In this century, an increasingly sophisticated student affairs profession has promoted the development of the whole person as an educational goal (Brown 1972; Miller and Prince 1976).

Institutions in this decade are changing again. First are societal changes, including uneven success with students from underrepresented groups in the education pipeline (Levine and Associates 1989), the burden of personal, corporate, and national debt (Frances and Harrison 1993), and an increasingly violent society (Siegel 1990). Second are changes in higher education itself, including a loss of public trust (Bok 1992), renewed demands for public accountability (Russell

1992), and budgetary constraints (Hines 1992). And third are changes in students, including an increasingly diverse student population (Gerald and Hussar 1992), increasing financial pressures on students (Astin et al. 1992), and growing interest in activism and community service (Levine and Hirsch 1990).

In response to these and other trends, institutions are launching new or enhanced efforts aimed at managing enrollments, promoting cultural pluralism and community involvement, garnering new sources of revenues, attempting to contain costs, and improving the quality of services to students. The role of student affairs professionals is central to and critical in many of these efforts.

Recognition of the importance of student affairs in these efforts on a growing number of campuses is leading to increased recognition of the congruity between the goals of student affairs and those of the institution at large. That is, serving students well is being rediscovered as an essential and defining goal of institutions of higher education. Efforts to increase enrollments of students from underrepresented groups, improve retention, and enhance academic achievement continue to grow on campuses throughout the country, creating opportunities for student affairs professionals to become fuller partners within institutions. A growing body of research documents the importance of these efforts as critical elements in institutional responses to changing conditions (Astin 1992; Green 1983). In particular, students' involvement in the collegiate experience is important, and the role that student affairs professionals play in promoting that involvement is critical (Astin 1985, 1992).

Thus, the traditional goals of student affairs—the development of the whole person, fostering involvement in the community, cultural pluralism, civic responsibility, and international understanding—are increasingly recognized as essential institutional goals. The potential for increased importance of student affairs continues to call for a revision of the role of student affairs professional. Student affairs professionals find themselves being integrators within the institution, integrating students' needs and traditional goals of student affairs on one hand with the varied needs of institutions responding to changing conditions on the other.

This role calls for an examination of student affairs programs and services and the skills needed by professionals. Perhaps most important, it establishes a new agenda for the preparation and continuing professional education of student affairs staff.

Changing Roles for Student Affairs
Responding to society's changing needs, student affairs has assumed a number of important roles within colleges and universities. The role has evolved from that of disciplinarian to coordinator and, more recently, to educator. The role of student affairs professional continues to build. Today, he or she serves as environmental scanner, milieu manager, market analyst, legal adviser, development officer, researcher, and quality assurance specialist.

The disciplinarian
Tutors responsible for student affairs at colonial colleges monitored students' behavior as guardians and catalysts of moral development. The concept of in loco parentis, which guided the relationship between students and the institution until recent years, is rooted in this concern for the moral life of young students (Moore 1990). College officials, acting in the place of parents, monitored students' social and moral development, often entailing punishing students for violations of any of hundreds of rules (Rudolph 1962). The student affairs portion of their work consisted of "a persistent emphasis on extracurricular religion, and also a considerable snooping into the personal lives of the student" (Cowley 1949, p. 20).

The goal of education in the colonial and pre–Civil War periods was to develop in young students a disciplined mind and soul, or, put another way, the goal of institutions was the development of a proper morality befitting an educated man. As a result, academic affairs and student affairs remained complementary goals of the faculty (Rudolph 1962; Ryan 1992).

Discipline was *the* student affairs approach in this period, but it began to change with students' increasing numbers and colleges' growing complexity. The notion that certain members of the college community would be responsible for shaping students' behavior and mete out discipline, however, took root at that time and remains with us to this day.

The coordinator
The rise of the U.S. university, embracing the evolution of the academic profession and the diversification of institutional mission, led to the establishment and expansion of the stu-

dent services profession. Perhaps the most influential of these trends was the increasing specialization of the faculty. Enlivened by opportunities to conduct research and to pursue scholarship, and with the growing diversification of faculty roles and fields of study, the academician of the late 1800s sought to be released of responsibilities associated with student life. The birth of the student affairs profession is usually marked by the appointment of the first personnel dean at Harvard in 1870 to handle the discipline of students (Shaffer 1987), taking the burden of student discipline off the shoulders of the newly appointed president, Charles William Elliot, who sought to free his time and that of his faculty for the pursuit of research and scholarship (Fenske 1989). Most aspiring universities and colleges soon adopted the practice of appointing a student personnel officer.

Co-curricular activities expanded after the Civil War, increasing the specialization and complexity of expanding colleges and universities. Seeking more stimulation than classrooms provided, students became involved in Greek letter societies, intercollegiate athletics, student publications, and literary and debating societies (Rudolph 1962), and, in response to the growing number of activities for students, institutions began to employ student services administrators to oversee and advise students on the activities that soon became an important part of college life.

Through much of this period, student affairs staff retained custodial responsibility over students' behavior while increasing their responsibility in an increasing number of activities. In addition, a number of student-related functions, including registration, advising, and counseling, became the province of many student affairs staffs (Cowley 1949).

The educator

The expansion of the student personnel movement after World War I occurred as a result of the acceptance of mental testing and counseling employed on a large scale by the Army during the war (Herr and Cramer 1979). The use of counseling and testing to assist an individual direct his or her talents and energies gained credibility and was adopted on campuses. The growth of this "personnel guidance" movement offered student affairs staff a greater degree of professionalism, and the development and application of new psychological and pedagogical theories supported the need for a student personnel function. The higher education community was beginning to accept the notion that noncognitive needs were important to the development of college students. Student health services, career placement, and intramural and intercollegiate athletics became part of an expanding and diversifying student affairs function on many college and university campuses (Brubacher and Rudy 1976).

Recovering from setbacks as a result of the depression, the student affairs profession prospered in the period preceding and just following World War II—a "golden age" for the student affairs profession (Deegan 1981)—when the identity of, emphasis on, and sophistication of student affairs functions increased. With publications by the American Council on Education describing college student personnel work, the philosophical basis of the profession sharpened, emphasizing the underlying spirit of "the personnel point of view":

> *The concept of education is broadened to include attention to the student's well-rounded development—physically, socially, emotionally, and spiritually, as well as intellectually. The student is thought of as a responsible participant in his own development and not as a passive recipient. . . . As a responsible participant in the societal processes of our American democracy, his full and balanced maturity is viewed as a major end goal of education and, as well, a necessary means to the fullest development of his fellow citizens* (American Council on Education 1949, p. 1).

Continued expansion of higher education in the 1960s and 1970s resulted in increased numbers of professionals with specialized responsibilities. Student affairs was called upon to provide a wider array of services in the areas of admissions, registration and records, financial aid, housing and food services, student activities, personal and academic counseling, orientation, and special services to a growing student body.

It was also a period of unrest among students, however, the aftermath of which proved to be a significant philosophical loss for the profession. In loco parentis, which institutions employed to guide their relations with students, was one of the many casualties of the period, along with the authority structures it fostered. Student personnel staff were caught in the uncomfortable position of needing to react to rapid changes among students without an organizing philosophy.

As a result, an increasingly diverse and complex profession sought to reestablish its theoretical base for professional practice and to embrace a philosophy to guide its efforts within the institution. Conceived in 1968, the Tomorrow's Higher Education Project of the American College Personnel Association emerged as an effort to define the mission and role of student affairs, the commitment to student development—the theories of human development applied to the postsecondary education setting—as a guiding theory, and the continued attempt to ensure that the development of the whole person was an institutional priority. With this activity, the student affairs profession sought to become more than a disciplinarian of student conduct or a coordinator of student activities and services and instead a human service professional responsible for shaping the development of students and student groups (Miller and Prince 1976).

The Role of Student Affairs Today

It is time to reflect on the changing role of student affairs and what is special about the profession (Clement and Rickard 1992). "Centering" the profession (see American Council on Education 1937, 1949) will be essential to meet the challenges of the 1990s. While the role and practice of the profession have evolved, the traditional goals of the student affairs profession remain strong.

The role of student affairs professional has continued to grow in support of institutional goals and needs, but in the role of supporting academic and institutional functions, student affairs has often been regarded as peripheral. Changing conditions in society, students, and higher education, however, demand new responses from institutions, and the involvement of student affairs in those responses is proving to be increasingly central as a result of increasing congruence between the goals of the institution and student affairs professionals—recruiting and retaining students, enhancing students' achievement, advising students about career development and placement, dealing with campus violence and intolerance, and creating inclusive campus communities. Student affairs professionals have the opportunity to be leaders in the achievement of institutional goals and, in so doing, integrating professional goals (student development) with institutional goals (organizational development).

The idea that student affairs professionals can serve as integrators within institutions is not new. The student personnel field must contribute to the institution as a whole and not solely to student development if it is to remain vital (Shaffer 1973).

If the developmental model emerged in part to supply a positive and less reactive approach to student life, then we must now move to the next step to incorporate a positive approach to institutional life and to respond positively to the issues facing our institutions (Smith 1982, p. 57).

As an integrator, the student affairs organization on campus shares the orientation of the three major campus groups— faculty, students, and administrators—and its position on the borders of those groups could be its greatest strength.

Our uniqueness as student personnel workers rests on our ability to fashion significant educational environments, using the resources, values, norms, and opportunities of the variety of constituencies on our campuses. To the extent that we are successful in our innovative work, we will be respected, not because of position, but as a result of the impacts we have on campus life. Truly, student personnel workers have the opportunities to be central figures for campus improvement in an era when resources must be perceived as newly combined rather than as new (Silverman 1980, p. 12).

Failing to accept the challenge to serve institutions and students effectively could prove costly for student affairs.

Student personnel work in the next 50 years will be called upon to perform even more significant functions than it has for the past 50. If it responds with creativity, ingenuity, and flexibility, there is no doubt of its future. If, however, it becomes the agent of the status quo and mere tradition, other fields will assume its work, and it will be reduced to performing mere housekeeping functions (Shaffer 1993, p. 167).

As integrators, student affairs professionals define their priorities and goals in terms of the institution and its students.

To serve effectively in that role within institutions, student affairs professionals will need to more successfully integrate the profession's philosophy, the efforts of the academic and student affairs worlds, and institutions with the society of which they are a part. Doing so will be challenging, but with the increasing recognition of the importance of student affairs in meeting the challenges of changing conditions, student affairs professionals can seize a special opportunity. But they will need to be ready to serve in a number of capacities not envisioned in the "traditional" role of student affairs.

The student affairs professional—today and in the future— must integrate the traditional student affairs roles as disciplinarian, coordinator, and educator with roles as environmental scanner, milieu manager, market analyst, legal adviser, development officer, researcher, and quality assurance specialist. As an integrator, the student affairs professional must focus attention on both students' and the institution's needs and seek to satisfy both. The function as an integrator will be increasingly important to the identification and achievement of institutional goals.

A CHANGING SOCIETY

The world of higher education is constantly changing, but the rate of change in the recent past is stretching institutions' resourcefulness. Higher education must respond to a society that is becoming more culturally diverse, is strapped with debt at a time when the cost of health care, welfare, criminal justice, and education continues to climb, is restructuring the way in which most tasks are carried out because of the increasing capacity of information technologies, and is becoming more violent. Each of these trends, shaping as they do the societal context for higher education, is leading to changes in institutional priorities, goals, and operations. By extension, these trends have important implications for the role of student affairs professionals (Allen and Garb 1993).

Continuing demographic evolution is leading to a society that is increasingly diverse, yet our ability to enable success for African-Americans, Latinos, Asian-Americans, and others is uneven. The extent of national, corporate, and personal debt shapes decisions and constrains opportunities throughout society. Demographic shifts—the graying of the population and regional variations in population growth and patterns of immigration—create problems and opportunities for institutions of higher education. The expanding capacity of information technologies is changing the ways in which we manufacture goods, educate people, and conduct business. And increasing violence brings a wide range of problems to campus.

A More Diverse Nation

The population of the United States continues to diversify. Minorities now make up 21.3 percent of the nation's population (Sagaria and Johnsrud 1991), and with higher birthrates and increasing numbers of immigrants from Central and South America, Asia, and Africa, minorities will continue to make up a larger portion of our citizens. While the nation's population grew by 10.2 percent from 1980 to 1990, growth rates of 11.7 percent for African-Americans, 38.7 percent for Native Americans, 104.7 percent for Asian-Americans, and 52.8 percent for Latinos were considerably higher (Hodgkinson 1991). On average, these groups are younger than whites. By 2010, 38 percent of the nation's youth will be made up of African-Americans, Latinos, Native Americans, and Asian-Americans, up from 30 percent in 1990 (Hodgkinson 1991). In some states—Hawaii, Texas, California, and New York, for example—

members of these groups will make up more than 50 percent of youth.

These figures suggest great potential for the enrollments of colleges and universities to become more representative of the nation's diversity. Nearly 3 million students from cultural or ethnic minority groups are enrolled in higher education (Carter and Merkowitz 1993), but our success in enabling students from underrepresented groups to enroll in college has not yet equaled that of whites. Despite increasing rates of graduation from high schools, African-Americans still fall behind whites in graduating (63 percent and 75 percent, respectively) (Solomon 1989). More disturbing is that the percentage of African-Americans who matriculate to colleges and universities continues to decline.

The Latino population in the United States is growing faster than that of African-Americans. While the number of Latino students in public education more than doubled from 1968 to 1986 (from 2 million to 4 million) (Orfield 1989), the rate at which Latino students graduate from high school (about 50 percent) and continue in postsecondary education (45 percent) shows no clear pattern of increase. While Latino enrollments in higher education continue to increase—up 10.7 percent from 1990–91 to 1991–92 for a total of 867,000 students (Carter and Merkowitz 1993)—these students represent a decreasing percentage of Latinos 18 and older (Orfield 1989).

As for African-American students, greater attention must be paid to the fact that Latinos increasingly are concentrated in low-income minority schools with poor records of graduation and achievement (Orfield 1989). Society must increase its efforts in concert with institutions of higher education to improve these schools if more Latino students are to complete high school and successfully make the transition to postsecondary education.

The fastest-growing minority group in the United States is Asian-Americans. As a group, Asian-Americans graduate from high school and attend higher education institutions at a higher rate than whites. Asian-Americans will likely grow to account for 7 percent of all students in higher education in the 1990s (Suzuki 1989). Despite the image of success, however, not all Asian-American students experience equally high rates of achievement. Patterns of success and college attendance are very different for students of Japanese, Korean, Chi-

nese, Vietnamese, and Pacific Island descent. Furthermore, despite increasing educational success, which often exceeds that of white students, Asian-Americans continue to face inequities in employment and income (Suzuki 1989). Efforts to cap enrollments of Asian-Americans at institutions could limit the ability to reduce these inequities.

Native Americans are a smaller but no less significant group on campus. From 1980 to 1990, the nation's Native American population grew 38.7 percent, compared to whites, which grew by only 3.9 percent (Hodgkinson 1991). In 1991, 114,000 Native American students were enrolled in institutions of higher education, up 10.7 percent from the previous year and representing 0.8 percent of all enrollments in higher education (*Chronicle* 1993b). Native American students are the least successful in persistence of all minority groups, facing particular problems with finances and academic preparation (Cibik and Chambers 1991).

During the 1980s, 6 million legal and some 2 million illegal immigrants settled in the United States (Stewart 1991). The largest portion of these immigrants were from Asia and Latin America; together, they made up one-third of the nation's population growth from 1980 to 1990. The ability of these recent immigrants to move into higher education and succeed is shaped by previous education and their immigration status. New immigration policies adopted in the late 1980s give preference to individuals with more education and training and will likely favor individuals with greater interest in and ability for higher education (Stewart 1991).

With regard to growth of these minority populations, recent reports by the U.S. Department of Education based on the 1990 Census project enrollments in grades 9 through 12 to grow 25 percent from 1991 to 2003 (Gerald and Hussar 1992). Similarly, college and university enrollments are projected to grow by 14 percent in the same period, fueled in large part by more high school graduates, increasing from a low of 2.5 million in 1991–92 to 3 million in 2002–3 (Gerald and Hussar 1992). Recent cuts in state funding and the inability of states to expand their institutions to meet demands are likely to mitigate this growth (Immerwahr and Farkas 1993).

Any growth will likely be uneven because states and regions expect very different growth patterns. The number of high school graduates, for example, is expected to decrease by as much as 17 percent in West Virginia and increase by as much

These figures suggest great potential for the enrollments of colleges and universities to become more representative of the nation's diversity.

as 60 percent in Nevada (Hodgkinson 1991), reflecting the general pattern of constant or declining population in the Northeast and Midwest and growth in the South and West.

The rate of growth for African-Americans, Latinos, Asian-Americans, and others and the age of each population will also create different trends for different regions. By 2000, African-Americans will constitute 13.1 percent of the U.S. population but 19 percent of the population in the South, 12 percent in the Northeast, 11 percent in the Midwest, and 6 percent in the West. In five states and the District of Columbia, African-Americans represent 25 percent or more of the population (Thomas and Hirsch 1989).

Most Latinos are concentrated in the Southwest and the metropolitan areas of Miami, Chicago, and New York, and each area has a different mix of Mexican-Americans, Cubans, Puerto Ricans, and other Latinos. Asian-Americans are concentrated in the Pacific Rim states, but like Latinos, substantial numbers of Asian-American students are found in certain other states and regions of the country.

Other Demographic Trends

The aging of the American population is another matter of concern for institutions of higher education. The fastest-growing age cohort is 35- to 44-year-olds: The baby boomers are reaching middle age. This group, already better educated than previous generations, is not enrolling in higher education as adults to the extent that the previous generation did. Perhaps the number of adults who actually attend college peaked in 1988 and their numbers will decline through the remainder of the century as these baby boomers move beyond their peak enrollment age (Brazziel 1989). The regions of the country where the decline in 18-year-olds is most severe (the Northeast and Midwest) will also see the sharpest decline in adult students (Solomon 1989).

This situation creates a double blow to institutions in the Northeast and Midwest: fewer adult students *and* fewer students of traditional age. Moreover, in these states, an aging population is less inclined to continue or increase funding for higher education (Astin 1992; Hines 1992). And to add to the dilemma, a large portion of the nation's institutions of higher education are concentrated in these regions. Thus we read about downsizing, closing, and merging institutions in the Northeast and Midwest at the same time we read of pressures to expand or develop new institutions in the South and West. Concern about the inability of state resources to fund needed expansion in California is fueling concerns that higher education is increasingly out of reach of many potential college students (Immerwahr and Farkas 1993).

The Burden of Debt

If the 1980s can be thought of as a spending spree, the 1990s will be remembered as the decade when the bills came due. From 1980 to 1990, the national debt increased from $900 billion to $3.2 trillion, and servicing the debt now consumes about 60 percent of federal personal income tax receipts (Frances and Harrison 1993). This level of debt continues to preclude additional government spending to lift the economy out of its doldrums.

As the federal government's spending on defense and health and social welfare entitlements grew in the 1980s, the burden of funding other programs typically shifted to state governments. The direct effects of the debt on the capacity of the federal government to spend and the consequent effects on strained state budgets have led to limited growth and real cuts in monies available for financial assistance for students and institutional subsidies. The extent of the national debt shaped decisions in the reauthorization of the Higher Education Act in 1992 to limit increases in Pell grants (Frances and Harrison 1993). Furthermore, strained state budgets contain less money for higher education, and appropriations for higher education in the states are declining (Hines 1992). Cuts in states like California, New Jersey, Maryland, Oregon, and Virginia have been profound; midyear budget cuts in many of these states and others have severely undermined programs and operations.

To make up the difference, public tuitions have increased in recent years on the assumption that students and families can find the resources to pay an increasing share of the cost of higher education. Consumers in the 1980s embraced new levels of debt, however: Mortgage debt increased precipitously as housing prices escalated, while general consumer debt increased substantially. Meanwhile, the nation's savings rate declined below that of other industrialized nations. As a result, the ability of students and families to cover the increasing costs of higher education out of savings, current income, or increased debt has all but evaporated, and the burden of debt is diminishing the capacity of governments, families, and students to cover the costs of higher education.

Technological Sophistication

The evolving capacity of information technologies continues to fuel economic restructuring, enable increased productivity, foster educational change and innovation, and cause considerable fear for those uncomfortable with change or, at least, the rate of change they face. Computer-aided design, manufacturing, and quality assurance have radically changed our ability to produce, management information processing enables the monitoring of vast international distribution systems, and data base analysis permits the almost instantaneous use of millions of pieces of information.

Few jobs are unchanged and many are in constant change because of the capacity of computers and information technologies. Vast numbers of manufacturing, clerical, and even middle management jobs have been lost to fewer, more productive workers using an array of computer equipment and information technologies. On the other hand, millions of service-oriented jobs have emerged for professionals able to fully employ the capacity of the new systems. We are emerging from a manufacturing nation as the world's premier exporter of highly professionalized services.

Campuses continue to remain on the cutting edge in the development, use, and application of information technologies. Campus offices are linked by fiber optics, and information—the product of the campus—is shared throughout the campus community instantaneously. Efficiencies in keeping records, analyzing data and information, and communicating help campuses to streamline operations and to evaluate the ongoing use, need for, and effects of programs and services.

The challenge for student affairs professionals is twofold. First, in working with students preparing for a technologically sophisticated world, student affairs professionals must understand the skills and abilities students need to succeed. Second, student affairs professionals must become proficient in the application of information technologies to deliver, evaluate, and improve services.

An Increasingly Violent Society

The United States has become an increasingly violent society, and, further, serious violent crime shows little sign of decline, especially in the nation's major metropolitan areas. Among developed nations, the United States experiences a substantially higher rate of violent crime and incarcerates a larger percentage of its population. Our colleges and universities are not immune from this violence.

We are surrounded by violence. "Real-life" cop shows on television elevate violent behavior to entertainment. Murders are nightly fare on the news, and child, spousal, and sexual abuse fill the agendas of talk shows. Increasing numbers of school students carry weapons, fearing for their safety in schools and on the streets.

The historical notion of the campus as sanctuary is giving way to the reality of the violence that permeates our society. Recent state and federal legislation requires institutions to report crimes and inform students and staff about security procedures. Thirty-six percent of respondents in one study reported being the victim of a crime during their college experience, and 10 percent reported having committed a crime (Siegel 1990). The study concludes that 80 to 85 percent of the crime is student-on-student and that alcohol is involved in more than half of the incidents.

Two areas pose particular challenges for student affairs professionals: hate crimes and acquaintance rape. The rate of hate crimes, including assault, harassment, and hate speech, is increasing substantially (U.S. Commission 1990), in all regions of the country and against all religious, ethnic, and sexual preference minority groups (Bodinger-Deuriarte and Sancho 1991). This level of ethnic violence is particularly troubling to institutions of higher education, which are specifically attempting to increase the cultural diversity of their campuses.

The level of acquaintance rape on college campuses continues to increase. While no firm figures are available, recent studies find that most college men and women have been involved in incidents of sexual aggression (Harrison, Downes, and Williams 1991). A study of freshmen finds that students bring violent behaviors with them to the campus and suggests that efforts to make students more aware of potentially violent behaviors and to provide educational interventions are essential to reducing violent activity (Stickel and Ellis 1991).

An Economy in Transition
The nation's and the world's economy is still in an often painful transition to a more interdependent world economy.

Despite efforts to establish economic spheres through, for example, the European Common Market and the North American Free Trade Agreement, the economies of the world increasingly depend on one another. Multinational companies, conglomerates, and holding companies serve the world by moving significant units or entire industries around the world to take advantage of economies in production (Barlett and Steele 1992). This "outsourcing" leads to computer-aided design in India, production in Indonesia, and warehousing in Mexico, with direction provided by smaller, more educated, and more productive U.S. headquarters staffs.

During the recession in 1990 and 1991, white-collar workers lost their jobs at rates comparable to those of blue-collar workers for the first time ever. Despite signs of recovery, layoffs continue to affect tens of thousands of workers each year, providing evidence of continuing restructuring. While the public increasingly is convinced that postsecondary education is the remaining route to the middle class (Immerwahr and Farkas 1993), choices of careers are changing. Interest in business careers has declined by half in the past several years (Astin 1992). Most careers for which substantial growth is projected (Hodgkinson 1991) require some postsecondary training but typically no more than an associate degree.

Restructuring is eroding the real or perceived ability of middle-class families (whose children form the core of college and university enrollments) to afford higher education. Record numbers of students indicate they selected their college for reasons related to finances (Astin 1992). Increasingly, families are worried about having access to higher education (Immerwahr and Farkas 1993).

An economy in transition highlights two implications for higher education. First, our role in preparing students to move effectively through a variety of positions and careers to capitalize on a changing economy will become even more essential. Second, the nation's capacity for education, training, and research and its applications is emerging as one of our strongest industries and enablers of economic development. New and resurging industries in the United States depend on highly intelligent, highly productive, and highly skilled workers. Energetic, creative, analytic, and technologically sophisticated individuals skilled in dealing with others are essential for growth. Contributing to the development of such individuals—including developing and enhancing programs to explore and adapt to changing careers, engaging in efforts to foster creative and analytic thought, increasing the capacity of individuals to flourish during ongoing change and capitalize on its opportunities—will be essential for the student affairs professional.

Summary
Societal change is constant and varied, and it directly and indirectly places pressure on institutions to adapt to it. The growing diversity of our population, demographic shifts, the pressures of debt, the demands of technological sophistication, increasing violence in our society, and the continuing transition of our economy demand the timely and dynamic responses of institutions.

Among the responses that institutions of higher education are making are those in which student affairs has the potential for leadership or significant participation. They include new or enhanced support services for diverse student populations, leadership in the management of enrollments, effective use of information technologies, attention to students' increasing concerns about their careers and the many burdens of debt, and attention to increasingly violent communities, including the campus. To the extent that student affairs professionals are able to take leadership in these areas and contribute meaningfully to students and to the institution itself, their role within the institution will be enhanced and strengthened. Their role will be to ensure that the goals of the student affairs profession will become integrated with those of the institution and vice versa.

THE NEW ACCOUNTABILITY FOR HIGHER EDUCATION

In addition to changes demanded by societal forces, other, more direct forces are pressuring higher education institutions to reexamine their relationship with society, their missions and purposes, and the ways in which they operate. The ever-changing political environment for higher education—shaped by a loss of public trust—demands that institutions become more accountable to government and society, that they demonstrate their success at enabling achievement among students, and that they operate with integrity in their relationships with students, faculty, staff, and the surrounding community. The pressure to justify comes at a time when financial support for institutions is shrinking and judicial scrutiny of institutional policies, procedures, and actions continues to grow. All in all, the new accountability for higher education asks institutions to do more with less money and perhaps less flexibility. As such, it is reshaping the relationship between society and its institutions of higher education.

Taken together, these changes are reshaping institutional missions, priorities, programs and services, and operational style. And student affairs professionals must be aware of the changes occurring and be prepared to respond to them.

The Loss of Public Trust in Higher Education

Over the years, higher education has been exempt from the oversight that society exercised over other institutions and agencies, predicated on a social contract that, as long as higher education served society's needs by providing high-quality instruction, research, and service with integrity, it would be afforded considerable autonomy. This stance reduced or eliminated pressures for change. More recently, however, decisions about higher education have become more politicized, and governmental involvement and oversight of the enterprise have steadily increased.

In the past several years, the public's confidence in higher education has eroded as a result of costs' increasing at a rate often twice that of inflation, scientific fraud, financial malpractice in the use of federal research dollars, conspiracy in tuition and financial aid (Bok 1992), opulent building programs, bidding for star faculty, athletic-entertainment programs (Winston 1992), and the fact that too many students are emerging from colleges and universities without sufficient skills and knowledge (Finn 1988). More and more, the public believes that institutions are increasingly irrelevant to society's major problems (Harvey 1992; Winston 1992).

We exist because citizens trust us with tax dollars; because students and parents trust us with hard-earned tuition dollars; because foundations and corporate donors trust us with grants and subsidies; because philanthropists trust us with gifts in their lifetimes and bequests in their wills. We exist because the people in the cities and towns we call "home" trust us to be good productive neighbors. And we are accountable to them all! (Cartwright 1992, p. 16).

To improve the public's opinion of higher education:

Within our colleges and faculties of arts and sciences we must make quality undergraduate education the top priority, and in our professional schools we need to play our full part in a national effort to overcome challenges that currently worry Americans—and justly so—about the future of their country (Bok 1992, p. 19).

To restore the public trust, institutions should accept the realities of their current situations, define institutional missions in relation to new economic and societal realities, find the fat in institutional budgets and cut it before someone else does, address public criticism as serious and substantive, and tell the success stories of higher education in this country (Harvey 1992).

Renewed Demands for Public Accountability
Efforts to restore public confidence will proceed in a climate where institutional flexibility is becoming constrained by measures to ensure increased accountability. Indicators of this growing accountability abound. Policy makers are interested in "light" faculty workloads (Russell 1992). Funding strategies reward or punish institutions on their ability to maintain quality and enable achievement among students (Garland 1991). A growing number of states require institutions to certify the fluency of all instructional personnel in the English language and to report to all students and employees information on crime statistics and security procedures. Institutions are asked

to respond to an increasing array of state policy initiatives aimed at economic development, including technology transfer, the development of research parks and incubator businesses, small business assistance, and customized job training. And everywhere is pressure for institutions to divulge operational details from the president's compensation to how promotion and tenure are decided. As a result, institutions find themselves accountable to more people in more ways.

Accountability to various federal statutes, regulations, and agencies is also growing. Recent federal legislation requires institutions to collect and report crime statistics and graduation rates for all students (student-athletes in particular) (the Right to Know Act and the Campus Security Act), to ensure accommodation for and equitable treatment of an increasing number of persons with disabilities (the Americans with Disabilities Act), and to be subject to greater state and federal oversight of institutions eligible for federal financial assistance (the Higher Education Reauthorization Act of 1992). New regulations are emerging to restore integrity in federally sponsored research programs, complementing existing requirements for institutions to manage student financial aid programs with integrity, provide equal opportunity in employment and student admissions, provide administrative due process, and ensure constitutional rights. The statutory and regulatory environment for higher education and the desire to avoid litigation shapes many institutional decisions (Cloud 1992). This accountability not only reduces flexibility, but also increases costs. Institutions spend an increasing amount of time and effort in such regulatory areas as alleged discrimination, student loan reports, and environmental management (Stern 1992). Other groups to whom higher education is accountable—regional and specialized accrediting associations, alumni, parents, and their surrounding communities—make increasingly greater demands about what they want from institutions.

Attention to state and federal statutes and regulations, to accrediting bodies, and to the needs and desires of more assertive alumni, parents, and students is causing institutions to look outside when making decisions. Student affairs organizations must become more aware of state and federal actions and their implications for institutional and student affairs practices, and they must integrate that awareness of external policies with existing institutional practices.

Other groups to whom higher education is accountable make increasingly greater demands about what they want from institutions.

The Focus on Outcomes

The publication in 1983 of *A Nation at Risk* (National Commission 1983) launched the educational reform era, and the publication of *Involvement in Learning* (Study Group 1984) turned educational reform to higher education. Various national and state studies offer recommendations to improve the quality of higher education, including new funding strategies, redesigned curricula, a reordering of faculty roles and responsibilities, and involvement of all members of the campus community in learning. Recommendations to improve the assessment of students' learning, found in a number of studies, have been institutionalized across the country in state policies, in the standards of regional and specialized accrediting associations, and in actions by the federal government. In a recent study, 82 percent of institutions have assessment projects under way, and nearly 40 states actively promote assessment (Hutchings and Marchese 1990).

Assessment, conducted within a broader agenda of fostering educational quality, is thus becoming a higher priority on college and university campuses. Tied as they are to finances, public opinion, and institutional marketing, the contributions of operational units to the achievement of outcomes are important elements in assessment. Student affairs professionals are participants in developing assessment programs in 81 percent of institutions reporting assessment activities (Hyman et al. 1988), and they have an opportunity to help shape assessment programs that reflect institutional missions— including goals for students' development—and are not solely based on academic achievement (Kozloff 1987). In their role of fostering campus involvement and "personalizing" the campus, student affairs organizations have the capacity to play a critical role in leading the reform of undergraduate education (McComas 1989).

Institutions of higher education have a mission to foster the development of students; marrying these efforts to an effective research agenda is essential if student affairs professionals are to be certain that students' achievement is assessed fully. The following questions should drive the research agenda:

1. How can we describe students in meaningful ways when they first enter college?

*2. How can we describe what students learn by the time
they leave the institution?*

*3. How can we describe the process of how students learn
and develop?*

*4. How can we show that what they learn is a result of
what we do?* (Hanson 1990, p. 277).

The New Economic Reality for Higher Education

Funding has been a topic of constant discussion for 30 years
in the literature on higher education. While the nature of the
discussion has changed over time, from strategies to fund
growth in the 1960s to managing retrenchment in the 1970s
(Mortimer and Tierney 1979) to investing in quality in the
1980s (Garland 1991), the issue endures. Today the discussion
once again centers on declining revenues. In 1991–92, state
appropriations for higher education declined for the first time
in 33 years (Hines 1992), and appropriations in 1992–93 declined further (Jaschik 1992). These decreases are in sharp
contrast to the latter half of the 1980s, when both public
and private institutions saw healthy increases in revenues
(Minter 1991).

With declining state appropriations, public institutions have
raised tuition to make up for lost revenues and increasing
costs. Tuition at public colleges and universities rose 10 percent in 1992–93 after rising 12 percent in the previous year,
on average (Evangelauf 1992). The rate for private institutions
was more modest, averaging 7 percent in each of those years.
Despite these increases in tuition, however, institutions experience internal budget cuts time and again. Cuts on many campuses have gone from mere belt tightening to draconian. Private institutions have not been immune, and independent
institutions have found limits to what students and families
are willing to pay. Tuition has been growing more slowly in
this decade than in the latter half of the previous decade.

As a result of changes in financial aid and rising tuition, the
affordability of higher education declined in the 1980s for
the middle class (McPherson and Schapiro 1990). The declining affordability of higher education is especially true for
minority students (Carter and Merkowitz 1993).

Insufficient sources of revenue have reopened debate on
redirecting institutional aid to student aid targeting dollars
for those who need them most. Some question a "high
tuition/high aid" strategy that many propose because the

political will to commit to high aid is in question (Mingle 1992). Cost containment and downsizing are becoming central in institutional planning (Simpson 1991; Waggaman 1991).

Judicial Influence

The increasing influence of court actions on institutional programs and practices matches that of other agencies external to the institution. Historically, U.S. courts have deferred to institutions in matters where academic judgment was deemed paramount (Fenske and Johnson 1990; Kaplan 1992). The result was little judicial intrusion in the operation of academic institutions.

The courts' involvement in campus issues has increased in recent years, however, as concern for civil rights has grown, governmental regulations have proliferated, and society has become increasingly litigious (Cloud 1992). The volume of litigation and the amount of time expended by institutional administrators on legal matters have increased greatly (Kaplan 1992). Institutional counsel are becoming more central players in making decisions and formulating policy (Samuels 1989), and an increasing amount of time is spent exploring the legal ramifications of decisions that might lead to litigation (Stern 1992).

Legal concerns shape the efforts of administrators. For instance, residence hall professionals confront issues of search and seizure, students' conduct, contracts, and liability for injuries; Greek life advisers deal with state antihazing laws; and all student affairs professionals are bound by confidentiality, due process, and equal treatment (Kaplan 1992).

For these reasons, institutions are increasingly concerned about their legal positions. Student affairs organizations, because of the variety of their functions and constituencies, are becoming increasingly aware of legal issues in their relations with students and campus organizations with regard to constitutional rights of free speech and freedom of the press, due process, discrimination, contractual rights and obligations, and liability. Knowledge of legal issues in these matters must inform institutions' practices in meeting students' needs.

Summary

While institutions are under pressure to adapt to changes in society, changes in higher education also demand responses by institutions. The world of postsecondary education has changed, and institutions find themselves increasingly accountable to state and federal laws, state and federal agencies, the public, and specialized constituencies inside and outside higher education. Doing so while public trust and public dollars are declining strains the capacity of institutions to respond effectively. As a result, institutions are calling on all units to contribute to reshaping institutional goals and priorities.

In large measure, these changes lead to changes in the goals, priorities, programs, and services of student affairs organizations. These changes have several implications:

1. Increasing attention to the political implications of policies and programs;
2. Increasing accountability in administrative practice and in the allocation and expenditure of funds;
3. Maximizing revenue sources by initiating or increasing fees for services;
4. Increasing attention to the rights of students and sources of potential litigation; and
5. Decreasing funds and eroding flexibility for operational units while demanding greater documentation of results.

A study of chief student affairs officers gives evidence of pressures professionals are under to maintain occupancy rates in residence halls, move functions to a fee-for-service basis, and minimize exposure to potential litigation (Sandeen 1991). Understanding external pressures and developing responses that meet students' and institutions' needs create new opportunities for student affairs professionals at the heart of institutional decision making.

Perhaps the most obvious and important areas of change affecting the role of student affairs are the increasing diversity of the student population and the evolving characteristics of college students. Much of our understanding of students—from student development theory, the student affairs professional's collegiate experience, and professional preparation—is based on types and characteristics of students that are often outmoded or narrowly drawn.

Today's student is more likely to be an older female who is a member of an underrepresented group and comes to college with different needs, values, and expectations from her predecessors. This student generally has multiple commitments, the campus is not her focus, and she prefers different learning situations from those typically offered on campus. She brings to campus different values, learning styles, expectations for career and life-style, educational expectations and motivations, and developmental needs. With much of our understanding about college students based on traditional students, the diversity of students and their needs today challenge institutional and student affairs practices.

Even as campuses evolve to meet the changing needs of students, the characteristics of all students are changing. The goals and values of students today are different from those of their predecessors (Dey, Astin, and Korn 1991; Howe and Strauss 1993). Changing student types and characteristics must be addressed to reshape student affairs, and attention to them must be integrated with institutional priorities. That integration holds great promise for the student affairs profession.

New Types of Students

The face of higher education is changing. More than half of college students are women, over 20 percent are members of underrepresented groups, nearly one-half of students attend part time, an increasing number have identified themselves as having a disability, and the median age of students is 28.

Women

Since 1979, women have outnumbered men in the total enrollment of colleges and universities. In 1988, women represented 54 percent of all higher education enrollments (Peng 1990), and in the next ten years, women will represent increasing percentages of the college population (Gerald and Hussar 1992). Efforts to address the needs of women in institutions that remain dominated by males, however, are relatively recent (Kuk 1990).

Increased participation by women in higher education and in fields once closed to women continues to challenge administrators. Women often lack role models in male-dominated fields, are subject to discrimination and sexual harassment, and continue to find "glass ceilings" on their careers. While expectations for sex roles are changing, men and women both find it difficult to resolve demands made by career, family, and traditional socialization.

This climate of change finds growing equality between the sexes in higher education and society (Hackman 1992), and women's preferences, attitudes, and values regarding careers have changed significantly over the past 25 years (Dey, Astin, and Korn 1991). Nevertheless, women rarely achieve equity with men in pay, despite higher achievement in college (Adelman 1991). Moreover, despite the fact that women account for more than half of college enrollments, women students report that campus cultures still tend to be white male in character (Kuk 1990). Campuses have generally failed to recognize gender differences in cognitive and affective development.

In addition to increasing numbers of women enrolling in higher education immediately after high school, substantial numbers of older women are returning to college. Because the reasons for returning are varied, the special needs of older women are similarly diverse, calling for flexible scheduling, child care, counseling in a wider array of domains, assistance in dealing with discrimination and harassment, and opportunities for exposure to role models and the development of mentor relationships.

Students from underrepresented groups
African-American, Latino, Asian-American, and Native American students, together with students of other cultural and ethnic groups, represented nearly 3 million students in 1991, and their numbers are expected to grow into the next century (Gerald and Hussar 1992).

Despite projections that participation rates of African-Americans in higher education would soon equal those of whites (Carnegie Council 1980), very little progress was made in the 1980s. Even with the institutionalization of policies on equal opportunity and affirmative action and active efforts at recruitment and retention, rates of African-Americans' participation and achievement have not increased substantially. Changing federal financial aid policies have made college less affordable to the economically disadvantaged, which includes large numbers of students from underrepresented groups. Lack of progress has been attributed to shifting policies on financial aid, poor high school preparation, and complacency (Brown 1991; Thomas and Hirsch 1989). As a result, colleges and universities are admonished to work more consistently and aggressively with school and community partners to increase graduation rates and continuation in postsecondary education (Carter and Merkowitz 1993; Hodgkinson 1991).

Recently, greater attention has been paid to the campus experiences of Latino students (Fiske 1988) and Asian-American students (Bagasao 1989). While expectations are similarly high for increasing rates of participation among these students, Latinos, members of certain Asian-American groups, and African-Americans often suffer from poor preparation in high school, financial barriers, and unwelcome campus climates that impede their ability to matriculate, maintain enrollment, and graduate. Student affairs organizations are critical in campus efforts to improve achievement among minorities. Institutions provide bridging experiences through student affairs work groups, seek to change the institutional environment, and provide special programs and services (Richardson and Skinner 1990).

Student affairs organizations should take the lead in sensitizing campuses to cultural diversity (Jones, Terrell, and Duggar 1991). With increasing evidence of hate crimes (U.S. Commission 1990), institutions will need to develop programs that create more inclusive campuses (Cheatham and Associates 1991). Research conducted in the 1980s confirms the significance of individual and cultural characteristics as critical and differentiating factors in development (Schlossberg, Lynch, and Chickering 1989). Newer models of student development seek to expand once ethnocentric student development models, but much remains to be done (Moore 1990).

Part-time students
With the expanded use of flexible curricula and scheduling, wider use of instructional media, and increasing numbers of nonresidential institutions, more students are able to attend college part time. Continuing pressures to upgrade skills and the inability of many to afford the costs associated with full-

time study also increase the number of part-time students, which now number about 43 percent of students enrolled in higher education (Peng 1990). With more adult students attending part time at all levels, discrete periods of education and work will likely blend in the future as lifelong learning becomes more necessary—and attractive—to students (Schlossberg, Lynch, and Chickering 1989).

Despite growing recognition of state, federal, and institutional aid policies, part-time students remain at a disadvantage in receiving financial aid, as many state and institutional aid dollars are available only to those pursuing full-time study. This practice increases the burdens on part-time students.

Flexibility in the design of academic programs and the delivery of student services characterizes the needs of part-time students. This flexibility should include variable class scheduling, opportunities for independent study and distance learning, flexible financial aid, and access to support services during evenings and weekends. Furthermore, support services part-time students need differ from those for full-time students. Efforts to help students address the competing pressures of work, study, and family and that seek to involve the student with others in the campus community are important to part-time students. Integrating the various needs of part-time students with the institution's priorities and goals is increasingly important in the attempt to retain students, creating opportunities for student affairs professionals.

Students with disabilities

Students with physical or learning disabilities are an increasingly important group on campuses today. The number of students entering higher education reporting disabilities has increased significantly, from 3 percent in 1978 to 9 percent in 1991 (Henderson 1992). The recent passage of the Americans with Disabilities Act has renewed societal and institutional commitment to equal opportunity for persons with disabilities in education programs and activities. The act also expanded the definition of "disability" to include learning disabilities, chronic health impairments, and alcohol and other drug dependencies—each with important implications for institutions and student affairs programs, including a variety of academic support services, group and individual counseling services, and health services.

Often institutions are least able to address learning disabilities, identified by 25 percent of those students reporting disabilities. The need is growing to employ experts in learning disabilities to assess and evaluate students' needs, develop strategies to promote their success, and advise faculty and others on methods and strategies to employ in teaching such students.

Students with disabilities bring various needs to campus, depending on the type, extent, and number of disabling conditions. To better accommodate students with disabilities, institutions must address physical barriers in and around campus, the availability and provision of learning assistance services like interpreters, recorders, and alternate testing programs, and sensitivity to a variety of challenging disabilities. Preadmission and orientation programs are particularly important for the adjustment of students who report disabilities, and all students who report disabilities might need support in developing social skills, leadership skills, and a positive self-concept (Hameister 1984). The student affairs professional can be instrumental in each of these areas in fostering a campus climate of inclusiveness and in assisting institutions to accommodate these students by organizing efforts to overcome the physical, instructional, and service barriers that face students with disabilities.

Students over 25 already make up more than one-third of college enrollments.

Older students

The aspirations, expectations, and needs of older students are significantly different from those of 18- to 24-year-old college students; that fact, coupled with the growing number of older students, is reshaping the efforts of institutions and student affairs organizations to address students' needs. Students over 25 already make up more than one-third of college enrollments. Many adults seek postsecondary education during a period of transition, and the events that precipitated the transition (loss of a job or divorce, for example) give rise to varying personal, educational, intellectual, and career needs for older students (Greenfeig and Goldberg 1984). The motivation, psychological development, academic readiness, and life/time commitments of older students are distinctive.

While the number of older students is not projected to grow (Solomon 1989), the types of older students and their reasons for seeking higher education will have important implications for institutions. Continuing economic transition affecting both service and manufacturing industries and causing companies as varied as IBM, Sears, GM, and Citibank to eliminate thousands of jobs will likely bring adults with some college experience back to campus for retraining. Similarly, the downsizing of the military is likely to create new demands for higher education. During the 1980s, educational incentives for joining the military increased competition for high school graduates. As a result, individuals leaving the military in the 1990s are likely to be high school graduates, to possess substantial training and technical skills, and to have access to college funds (Hexter and El-Khawas 1988).

Adults typically enter higher education with a high level of motivation and specific educational and career goals. For many, the transition to the college environment can be difficult, however. Adults exhibit different learning styles, academic and social concerns, and family role obligations, but institutional responses, including career development counseling, role and stress management, general counseling and academic advising, flexible scheduling, and financial aid, have only slowly evolved (Schlossberg, Lynch, and Chickering 1989).

Recognizing the needs of adult students in higher education creates opportunities and challenges for institutions and their student affairs organizations. With attention to the development of students regardless of age, student affairs professionals can be instrumental in integrating the needs of adult learners with the goals and priorities of institutions. An entry course for adult learners would be a good first step:

> *Adults need an introductory learning experience that provides an opportunity for a realistic self-appraisal of their potential as adult learners, the achievement of a sense of belonging . . ., and a deeper understanding of higher education in general and liberal education in particular* (Steltenpohl and Shipton 1986, pp. 637–38).

Summary

Addressing the needs of an increasingly diverse student population in higher education has captured much attention. Efforts that are increasingly routine include conveniently scheduled and accessible support services, thorough orientation, special services for a variety of student groups, modification of the campus climate to promote inclusiveness, modified and reshaped programs and services to meet students' needs, and continuing professional development of student affairs staff. These changes have several implications for student services:

1. Greater attention to the particular needs of women of all ages as they enter more varied academic programs and careers and define roles in new ways, including broader attention to differences in the way men and women learn, design and delivery of curricula, development of women's centers, policies regarding harassment, assertiveness training, and child care.
2. Attention to the barriers of achievement for a variety of students from underrepresented groups, including students' previous academic preparation, institutional climate, and design and delivery of curricula. It might also include policies and practices to foster inclusiveness, programs and services to serve cultural or ethnic groups, transition programs, mentoring, and learning and interpersonal styles.
3. Flexibility in the delivery of student services to part-time students and the incorporation of issues important to non-campus-based students with multiple commitments in the design of programs.
4. Identification of learning assistance programs and services for students with disabilities, including an advocate for students with disabilities.

Attending to the various needs of students is increasingly important to institutions and thus to student affairs professionals. Integrating the needs of the wide range of today's students with institutional goals and priorities provides both a challenge and an opportunity for student affairs.

New Characteristics of Students
Regardless of age, ethnic group, or gender, students of the 1990s are different from their predecessors. Nowhere are those changes more evident than among post–baby boomers—those born in the 1960s and 1970s who are now coming to college.

These students are alternately described as uninspired and irresponsible or committed to the improvement of society. Popular books and novels, such as *13th Gen: Abort, Retry, Ignore, Fail?* (Howe and Strauss 1993) and *Generation X* (Coupland 1991), suggest that incoming college students are uninspired, materialistic, irresponsible, and feeling more entitled than accountable. This generation of students, the first who cannot expect to do as well as their parents, might simply be trying to come to terms with what might be lost. Others (Levine 1993) find in this generation of students an increasing commitment to improving society, to working hard to engage themselves in the community, and to seeking more satisfaction from making a meaningful contribution than in making money.

Whether students are more or less engaged on the one hand and more or less accountable for their actions on the other presents different challenges for institutions and student affairs professionals. What might be more important, however, is a recognition that students of the 1990s present different needs, expectations, values, and outlooks from their predecessors. Students mirror a changing society through the characteristics they bring to campus, among them financial pressures, academic underpreparation, participation in behaviors that put health at risk, and commitment to personal and social development.

Financial pressures

Concerns about the cost of higher education and the ability to afford an education have always been part of the campus climate. Recent increases in tuition, however, expanding gaps between what families can afford and the cost of higher education, have not been matched by increases in financial aid. And students increasingly are concerned about meeting college costs. The cost of attendance is an increasingly important consideration in choice of college, and 30 percent of students in one study indicated that they selected their freshman college based on low tuition (Astin et al. 1992). A record number of students (17.4 percent) reported a major concern about being able to afford college, and more students are living at home and are expecting to work during college (Astin et al. 1992). African-Americans are more likely than whites to select colleges because of low tuition (Dey, Astin, and Korn 1991). A study completed for the California Higher Education Policy Center found an increasing recognition that postsecondary education is essential for entry to or maintenance of middle-class status—matched by an increasing fear that such education is becoming more unattainable each year (Immerwahr and Farkas 1993).

While research in the late 1980s reported that students increasingly were choosing academic programs based on relative anticipated incomes and seeking more lucrative fields like business (Mohrman 1987), interest in other fields is growing as the "guaranteed" return on such programs diminishes. Interest in business careers has declined since 1988 (Dey, Astin, and Korn 1991), and interest is increasing in education and health careers that are traditionally more stable during economic fluctuations and allow more personal contributions to society's welfare (Green 1989).

Academically underprepared students

Poorly prepared students are one of the largest and fastest-growing subgroups in higher education (Astin 1984). Increasing numbers of freshmen believe they need to improve their reading and study skills (43 percent in 1990) and expect to seek out tutoring (15.9 percent in 1990) (Dey, Astin, and Korn 1991). Faculty also report a decline in students' skills. Three-quarters of faculty surveyed in one study felt that students in general were seriously underprepared in basic skills (Carnegie Foundation 1989).

Many students, recently attracted to higher education, were poorly prepared in high school. While large numbers of nontraditional students need additional academic support, increasing numbers of traditional students have also been found to need remedial programs (Astin 1992). In recognition, institutions increasingly have tried to create and expand academic support programs.

Despite declining academic skills, increasing numbers of students expect to be elected to honor societies and aspire to advanced study beyond the bachelor's degree (Dey, Astin, and Korn 1991). The potential disparity between ability and aspiration for many students could become an important part of student advising and counseling in college.

In addition to remedial programs designed to address basic study skills in math and writing, poorly prepared students need educational and career counseling that seeks to match ability and aspirations. Developing efforts to address an increasing number of students who need help in developing skills is becoming increasingly important in institutions' efforts to retain students. Helping students to reasonably assess their abilities and develop career and life goals accordingly will become an increasing challenge for student affairs professionals.

Engaging in health-risking behaviors

For some time, student affairs professionals have been responsible for the education, counseling, and discipline of students in the areas of alcohol, drug use, and sexual activity. An emerging focus on the health risks associated with such behaviors is capturing greater attention on campuses.

The fact that students drink on campus is not new, but conflicting evidence of students' use and abuse of alcohol calls for informed responses from institutions. The consumption of beer and wine continues to decline, and only about half of students report occasional or frequent drinking (Astin et al. 1992), down from nearly three-fourths of students in 1981–82. In a recent national survey, however, 42 percent of students reported engaging in binge drinking, and 23.2 percent reported that they had experienced academic difficulties as a result of their drinking (Presley and Meilman 1992). Furthermore, alcohol is a factor in most incidents of violence on campus (Siegel 1990).

While much attention in recent years has been focused on alcohol use, the use of drugs continues to be a problem on campus. A recent survey found relatively high levels of use among college upperclassmen, particularly males (Robinson et al. 1993). When asked about use in the previous year, over 40 percent had used marijuana, 20 percent tranquilizers, 19 percent narcotics, 18 percent cocaine, and 14 percent hallucinogens.

These figures are alarming for student affairs professionals who have worked for years to establish education, intervention, and treatment programs for alcohol and other drugs. Students rarely begin alcohol or drug use in college; for many, serious use and dependency developed before matriculation. Dealing with the consequences of such behavior, particularly on residential campuses, remains a concern for student affairs professionals, and they will feel pressure to evaluate and redesign efforts to more effectively address the use of alcohol and other drugs (see Presidential Task Force 1992 for a discussion of institutional policy and practice, preventive education, and strategies for intervention and treatment).

A second area of concern is HIV/AIDS and college students' sexual behavior. AIDS has become the sixth leading cause of death among 15- to 24-year-olds, and studies of incidence rates on campus project that approximately 2.5 per 1,000 students would be HIV positive (Gayle et al. 1990). In a study of students at the University of Massachusetts, 85.5 percent of students stated that they did not feel very or at all susceptible to becoming infected with HIV, despite varying knowledge of responsible sexual habits (Bustamante 1992).

Despite efforts to increase students' awareness of the need to engage in responsible behaviors, students still engage in activities that present considerable risks to their health. The need for continuing efforts to educate and counsel students in these areas and in understanding emerging research is essential for student affairs organizations. An alcohol/drug and HIV/AIDS prevention program for campuses should include several components:

1. Increasing students' sense of vulnerability to HIV infection;
2. Recognizing that heavy use of alcohol and drugs signals a person who is at risk for HIV infection;
3. Refusing to accept alcohol and/or drug intoxication as an excuse for inappropriate or risky behavior;
4. Combatting peer pressure and supporting responsible behavior; and
5. Tailoring the message to the distinct characteristics of the target group (Wright, Watts, and Garrison 1993, p. 306).

Commitment to personal and social development
While the ability to find jobs and succeed in a career remains a strong concern for students, evidence suggests that students' interest in their own personal development and in social and political issues is growing. Entering freshmen are increasingly interested in developing a meaningful philosophy of life as a major goal (Dey, Astin, and Korn 1991). Similarly, a majority of students report involvement in community service activities in high school and an expectation of continuing such activities in college (Astin et al. 1992; see also Delve, Mintz, and Greig 1990 and Morse 1989 for advice on strategies to implement and manage effective community service programs).

Despite such commitment to society, students in general and students of color in particular continue to become less sanguine about race relations and the capacity of the nation to accept its cultural diversity (Astin et al. 1992), suggesting that efforts to foster inclusive campus climates and to prepare students to work effectively in a multicultural society remain important to student affairs organizations.

When Dreams and Heroes Died (Levine 1980) found students self-absorbed, optimistic about their own future but pessimistic about the nation as a whole, and generally unable to name a hero to emulate. A decade later, those characteristics changed, and evidence increasingly suggested that students were becoming more optimistic about the country, more socially involved and active, and much more likely to be able to identify a hero to emulate—more often than not a member of their community (Levine and Hirsch 1990). More students look for jobs upon graduation that will allow them to make a social contribution.

Others have also found a recent resurgence in political and social activism (Dey, Astin, and Korn 1991). While active involvement in traditional politics (such as working on a political campaign) continues to decrease, more than a third of students now report that they participated in organized demonstrations before matriculation. Students might be disenchanted with traditional politics but increasingly engaged in developing positions and advocating for them on issues like the environment, race relations, and health.

Colleges and universities should heed these changes in students' interests and activities (Levine and Hirsch 1990). Political activism on campus is reviving, and colleges must plan carefully for increasing social engagement. After years of attention to students focused on success in a career, one wonders whether campuses are prepared to help students understand skills and knowledge needed for civic engagement, whether sufficient opportunities for social service and political action are available, and whether institutions are ready for increasing demands for students' involvement in institutional governance. Campuses must be able to capitalize on the educational opportunities presented by such activism and tolerant of the pressures it could place on them. Student affairs professionals must help their institutions find a workable balance, just as they must find a balance between their roles as disciplinarians (keeping the campus quiet) and educators (capitalizing on an opportunity to learn).

Summary

Even as institutions attempt to assimilate new groups of students, students in general are changing. Students of the 1990s exhibit different goals and values, expectations for education and a career, and interests. Students today are more concerned than ever about financing a college education and the ability to achieve success in a career, but optimism about society, perhaps because of their increasing social and community involvement, is on the rise. Concerned about their academic preparation, students today might have more unrealistic expectations about their academic success. Students' knowledge about health-risking behaviors is growing, but their choices to engage in them are troubling.

These changes in students create opportunities and challenges for student affairs organizations. For many, the resurgence of interest in community and personal development will excite professionals long concerned about students' vocationalism and materialism. Student affairs professionals knowledgeable about students' current needs, interests, and expectations stand in a position to lead campus efforts to serve students who are more active, involved, and committed to community and social development. They might also serve as an advocate for students whose educational preparation does not yet equal their aspirations. Assuming leadership in reshaping campus efforts to serve students' needs can result in more effective and productive academic and student affairs programs.

For student affairs organizations, these changing needs, interests, and values of students suggest:

1. Increased efforts aimed at helping students improve basic skills and establish reasonable expectations for life and career;
2. Focused attention on the needs of students (before college as well as matriculants) to understand the costs of higher education and strategies to defray those costs (with more students at their "second" choice, efforts to engage and involve them could be different);
3. Increased attention to the development and management of community service programs and opportunities to learn from service to others;

4. Increased efforts to train and develop student leaders for effective engagement in institutional and community governance;
5. Increased attention to students' need for health-related information and efforts to effectively shape their alcohol and sexual behaviors;
6. Increased efforts in career planning and placement.

Addressing the needs of students whose characteristics, needs, and values are changing at the same time the range in the types of students is expanding will be challenging. Student affairs professionals, however, will be increasingly important in developing comprehensive institutional strategies to deal with the diversity of students.

CHANGING INSTITUTIONAL STRATEGIES

Much attention in the middle to late 1970s was given to the usually dire results to be expected as a result of demographic and financial trends, changing student clienteles, and eroding conditions for higher education, with the 1970s and 1980s characterized by "reduction, reallocation, and retrenchment" (Mortimer and Tierney 1979). Yet the latter half of the 1980s turned out to be strong for higher education. Enrollments continued to grow, new groups of students were attracted, and a greater portion of high school graduates sought to enroll in higher education. State appropriations grew at a healthy rate, often fueled by an interest in preserving and enhancing quality in public higher education. Students and families endured increasing tuitions, believing that institutions whose tuitions were higher delivered greater quality. Real or perceived growth in family incomes and expanding state financial aid programs helped to meet the increasing costs. In short, resilient institutions met students and families willing to invest in higher education.

Today, decreasing state appropriations, steady or declining family incomes, and a growing interest in value put pressure on institutions to control costs.

Today, decreasing state appropriations, steady or declining family incomes, and a growing interest in value put pressure on institutions to control costs. Coupled with continuing concerns about the demographics of higher education, doomsayers echo earlier dire predictions for the future of higher education. The resilience with which institutions have responded to previous periods of stress will stand them in good stead in facing the realities of the 1990s.

Based on a premise that organizations seek to grow, colleges and universities have employed strategies to preserve or resume growth when faced with conditions that would diminish that prospect (Leslie and Miller 1974). Institutions should attempt to revitalize themselves through several strategies:

1. *The introduction of a new good or grade of good already in use.* If the degree is one of the goods produced in higher education, the amount of time and the types of degrees have changed to meet new market forces over the years—the awarding of baccalaureate degrees for teachers, associate degrees, and external degrees, for example. More recently, institutions have structured programs for part-time students, continuing professional education, and the awarding of associate and baccalaureate degrees as a credential and a wider range of fields.

2. *The introduction of a new method of production, i.e., a new type of labor-saving machinery.* Over the years, classes have grown in size, more graduate teaching assistants have been used, and the media have been used more extensively in higher education. Credit for previous experience and weekend programs are examples.
3. *The opening of new markets.* This strategy has probably been the most used innovation in higher education. We have a long history of becoming more egalitarian in the types of programs offered and students attracted. Various new student clienteles have become increasingly important to institutions.
4. *The employment of a new source of supply production factors.* Institutions have long sought financial resources from a variety of sources, including churches, federal, state, and local governments, and auxiliary enterprises. Most recently, institutions have sought voluntary gifts from friends, alumni, corporations, and foundations. Similarly, increased management of funds and internal accountability for the use of funds have been used to get the most out of resources available.
5. *The reorganization of an industry, several industries, or part of an industry.* Higher education institutions have sought to form consortia, joint research institutes, and collaborative efforts with business and industry and other organizations (Leslie and Miller 1974, pp. 24–25).

Today, institutions are revitalizing and reorienting their efforts in the face of external pressures by increasing emphasis on principles of quality management, using information technologies, refining the management of enrollments, attempting to attract private monies (for public colleges) and public dollars (for private colleges), containing costs, and forging new partnerships with business and public education. These strategies are emerging from aggressive institutional planning and management. The extent to which they are successful in maintaining an institution's vitality will determine institutions'—individually and collectively—ability to survive into the next century.

Principles of Quality Management

Concerns about enrollments and pressures to refocus energies, scale back size, and increase accountability to a variety of constituencies argue for more effective management in higher education. As a result, the application of management theories, practices, and strategies to higher education has grown. Borrowed from business, the growing body of references on academic management leads to increasing sophistication in academic leaders' management.

Like the institutions of which they are a part, student affairs organizations are more systematically applying principles of management. The growing body of literature on management in student affairs routinely addresses the allocation and management of resources (Barr 1988), program review and evaluation (Brown 1985; Gordon and Weist 1988; Ludeman and Fisher 1989), the development and supervision of professional staff (Woodard and Komives 1990), management issues in general (Barr, Upcraft, and Associates 1990; Delworth, Hanson, and Associates 1989; Sandeen 1991), and management skills needed for effective leadership (Clement and Rickard 1992).

The increasing attention to management in colleges and universities is not without its detractors. While for some, increasing attention to professional management brings much-needed efficiencies to campuses (Waggaman 1991), others remind us that education is a business unlike all others and cannot be made to focus solely on the bottom line (Rollin 1989).

Considerable interest in Total Quality Management (TQM) or Continuous Quality Improvement (CQI) is growing on many campuses. These strategies of quality management seek to improve the efficiency and effectiveness of colleges and universities. Quality management seeks to engage the talents of the campus fully in making certain internal and external customers of all activities are satisfied. Organizations that adopt quality management will have:

- Constructive competition
- Shared values and unity of purpose
- Collaboration on broad issues
- Simultaneous and synergistic planning
- Emphasis on responsibility to contribute
- Decentralized partnerships built upon situational management
- Team accountability
- Constancy of purpose

- Win-win resolution of conflicts through conflict management and
- Probably most important, a superior professoriat, student body, and administration (Cornesky et al. 1991, p. 9).

In 22 institutions that have implemented TQM, a number of student affairs functional areas were improved, including management of enrollments, outcomes assessment, career planning and placement, and housing procedures (Seymour 1991). In implementing TQM, institutions found that initial investments in training, study, and evaluation resulted in increased efficiency and effectiveness over time.

Quality management holds great promise for student affairs. First, because student affairs organizations are focused on students and quality management refocuses institutions' efforts on customers, primarily students, attention to traditional goals of student affairs is likely to increase. This is not to say that in quality management goals for student affairs will not have to be revised and focused—simply that with all units in an institution working cooperatively to establish goals focused on customers and evaluating efforts directed at their satisfaction, student affairs professionals will be able to provide leadership. Employing an approach of quality management, student affairs organizations can sharpen planning and management while maintaining their commitment to the development of students.

Second, as a strategy to evaluate and rank student affairs programs, principles of quality management can enable student affairs professionals to focus their efforts and develop confirming data to identify those efforts most essential to students' satisfaction. In tough fiscal times, student affairs organizations can take the lead in effectively evaluating efforts, enhancing those that best serve students or reducing or eliminating those that do not.

Information Technologies

Continuing advances in information technology hold great promise for institutions in the quality and effectiveness of management, information about students, design and delivery of curricula, and the extent and quality of interaction between students in and out of class. Expansion of campus fiber optics systems, use of Internet and Bitnet, integration of information processing in the classroom, use of custom-designed textbooks and instructional materials, the capacity for efficient management, and the availability of information about students fill the agendas of campus meetings and the journals and newsletters of professional organizations.

In student affairs organizations, the expanding use of information technologies leads to the ability to employ more sophisticated information about students and the institution to design programs and services, to increase productivity in management, planning, and information processing, and to design and deliver services by phone, computer, and media (Baier 1993).

Essential to the design, delivery, and evaluation of any program or service is the effective management and use of information. First, through the collection and analysis of data about students and programs, student affairs professionals are able to learn more about students' needs, characteristics, program use and effectiveness, and the like. Student affairs professionals should develop strategic information about students, staff, programs, curricula, facilities, equipment, and finances; put in a usable form, such information can be used for creative solutions to problems or to capitalize on opportunities for new efforts. Perhaps most important, it can assist student affairs organizations to target efforts for maximum impact.

Second, use of information technologies can greatly increase the capacity of student affairs organizations to handle the volume of information and communication involved in student affairs. Automated office systems and integrated student information systems encompassing admissions, academics, financial aid, discipline, student development activities, placement, and alumni records can vastly expand the ability of student affairs professionals to address individual needs and to develop a sophisticated understanding of students.

Finally, information technologies offer the opportunity for the delivery of student affairs programs and services with fewer people. Telephone menus to link questions with answers and services, information kiosks, computer-based guidance systems and assessment, data bases to provide timely information (about internships and employment, for example), and interactive videoconferencing to off-campus centers or to a student's home can expand the productivity of student affairs professionals in serving students.

Student affairs professionals can reach out and match a student's needs with academic and developmental programs and services through better information, and the goals of enrollment management can be better achieved through the employment of information technologies (Erwin and Miller 1985). The effective use of technology can help student affairs professionals better enable the development of students through ongoing analysis of the use, outcomes, and evaluation of programs and services (Baier 1993).

Refining Enrollment Management
Enrollment management involves:

> . . . a host of functions that cross divisional lines, including clarification of institutional purpose, program development, marketing and recruitment, financial aid, orientation, and retention. . . . As a process, enrollment management helps institutions: (1) develop a keener awareness of their purpose and character in relation to the student marketplace; (2) improve ties to prospective client groups; and (3) attract students into and through the institution (Baldridge, Kemerer, and Green 1982, p. 27).

As a set of strategies, enrollment management provides a systematic approach to attracting, retaining, and graduating students. As institutional efforts to effectively manage enrollments have expanded, all members of the campus community have become more actively involved in the process. Continuing concerns about the number of students and more specific concerns about the ability of institutions to attract, retain, and graduate students from underrepresented groups are troubling issues for most institutions.

In the 1980s, a growing body of literature established the importance of efforts to improve the recruitment and retention of students and their achievement. A study of the role of student services in eight underenrolled institutions demonstrated that the investment in efforts could reap benefits in retention (Green 1983), and a study of college presidents found that presidents regarded the chief student affairs officer to be critical to recruitment and perceived him or her to possess considerable skill and expertise in this area (Kinnick and Bolheimer 1984). More recent work demonstrates that student affairs professionals' increasing involvement in campus means students are more likely to remain enrolled, to develop, and to achieve (Astin 1992; Pascarella and Terenzini 1991). The students most likely to graduate from institutions are those already enrolled; reducing attrition is the easiest way for institutions to maintain healthy enrollments (Levine and Associates 1989).

More recently, scholars have attempted to determine the effect of specific programs on reducing attrition among students. Financial aid, college survival programs, and extended orientation programs are important to persistence (McIntire et al. 1992; St. John, Kirshtein, and Noell 1991; Upcraft, Gardiner, and Associates 1989). Students actively engaged in their campuses are more likely to achieve and persist (Astin 1992). (See Hossler 1991 for direction in evaluating recruitment and retention programs.)

Yet as financial pressures worsen, student affairs organizations and their programs often suffer disproportionately (Cage 1992). In an attempt to downsize programs and balance strained budgets, institutions often cut student affairs budgets and programs designed to address the varying needs of a diverse population to maintain the vitality of the institution's academic core. Such a strategy, however, could prove counterproductive, given the potential for a crisis in enrollments in many institutions; a viable student life component could determine the very survival of some institutions (Baldridge, Kemerer, and Green 1982).

Given the importance of retention to an institution's viability, chief student affairs officers should lead the effort to understand why students leave, where they go, and what efforts lead to their retention (Shay 1984). Such an effort was the successful Intentional Student Development and Retention Consortium, involving 12 colleges and universities in the Northeast, which brought faculty and student affairs professionals together to develop effective strategies (Stodt 1987b). The importance of student affairs professionals' efforts to recruit and retain students and to manage enrollments cannot be understated.

Broadening the Resource Base

While continuing to court their traditional supporters, colleges and universities are actively seeking funding from other sources. And institutions are developing an increasing array of programs and activities to generate additional revenues.

While state appropriations for higher education have dipped, private giving for higher education continues to grow.

In fiscal year 1991, private giving to higher education amounted to $10 billion (Council for Aid 1991). Annual giving and capital campaigns are part of every institution's revenue development plan. Major campaigns, seeking to generate hundreds of millions of dollars, are not unusual among a growing number of both public and private institutions.

More recently, the debate over whether to subsidize institutions or students has been renewed. Subsidies for students rather than for institutions could be an effective strategy, but the level needed to make the system work could be too great (Mingle 1992).

Regardless of funding from the major sources of revenue, institutions are seeking to develop new, albeit smaller, sources of revenue. Some approaches, like debit cards for campus food and other services that provide flexibility for students and controlled profit margins, are more profitable ways to perform current functions. Others, such as sports, music, and avocational summer camps, elderhostels, training and conference programs, and personal enrichment programs and services, are newer ventures. While their most important function is perhaps to use campus facilities more fully, they can also be a source of revenue, create interest in eventual enrollment for a student, and increase the institution's generation of revenue in the local community. Other activities, such as licensing and marketing the institutional logo or trademark, are pursued primarily for the revenue they generate. Institutional activities contributing to economic development are leading to the creation of research parks and business incubators, hotels or other conference facilities, and the development of campus facilities to house private ventures serving the college community.

Not all efforts designed to increase an institution's revenue base are viewed positively. More and more institutions are competing for private dollars, and competition for public dollars is heating up. But the many institutional activities designed to generate revenues provide opportunities for student affairs organizations. Today's student is tomorrow's alumnus or alumna, and interest is growing in fostering the desire to continue supporting the institution even before graduation. In many institutions, student affairs professionals are integrally involved in fund raising and alumni activities. Student affairs professionals could be instrumental in identifying and organizing students to cultivate and solicit support among alumni.

More specifically, student affairs professionals could be involved in fund-raising activities among classes, associations of parents, and the like. Likewise, many student affairs organizations are working with private funds that have been made available to support typical student services, such as named and general scholarship funds, funds to support cultural activities, and capital funds to construct or renovate residence halls, arts centers, and student activities buildings.

Cost Containment
Even as institutions seek to broaden their sources of revenue, they seek to contain costs as much as possible. While cost containment is a goal more than a strategy, increasing attention is paid to the ability to maximize revenues while minimizing or avoiding costs (see, e.g., Waggaman 1991 and Zemsky and Massey 1990).

Institutions should employ certain principles as they seek to reduce the scope of their operations:

1. Strong organizations often need retrenchment as much as declining organizations.
2. An institution's mission should be reconsidered before retrenchment is considered.
3. Retrenchment must consider the possibility of growth.
4. Decreasing expenses has a more predictable impact on financial resources than increasing revenues.
5. Across-the-board reductions should be minimized.
6. More revenues often mean more costs.
7. Issues of quality should be as important in retrenchment as issues of revenues and costs (Chabotar and Honan 1990, pp. 30–31).

Student affairs organizations in institutions embarking formally or informally on cost containment might be greatly concerned over potential cuts in the student affairs budget. That concern can be minimized by organizations that can clearly demonstrate their efforts to be cost-effective, particularly efforts that lead to students' achievement and persistence, or by organizations that explore other sources of revenue. Institutions looking to contain costs might ask faculty to reassume advising and counseling, however, roles currently performed by student affairs professionals (Lazerson and Wagener 1992). In such situations, student affairs professionals must articulate their strengths and successes and be willing—along with others in the institution—to reassign or eliminate some efforts.

Building Partnerships

For years, colleges and universities have nurtured relationships with business, industry, and other schools in six broad areas of collaboration: (1) concurrent enrollment programs; (2) enrichment, compensatory, and motivational partnerships; (3) academic alliances and other teacher-to-teacher partnerships; (4) preservice teacher education and professional development efforts; (5) tutoring and mentoring programs; and (6) partnerships for school improvement or restructuring (Greenberg 1991). Partnerships between higher education and elementary and secondary schools, for example, generally seek to strengthen teaching and learning and improve access to postsecondary education. Such relationships recently have become more frequent and formal as all partners seek to re direct efforts, borrow expertise, and deal more effectively with complex social and economic problems.

Partnerships between business and higher education have grown out of collaborative efforts to conduct research and expand the frontiers of technology. Recently, business and industry and institutions of higher education have seen that collaborative efforts like research projects, cooperative education, sharing equipment, personnel, and facilities, and job training and professional development are becoming increasingly important to the future vitality of both. In working together, however, collaborators need to have realistic expectations, ongoing administrative support, a focus on satisfaction for consumers, and insulation from the other organization's internal politics (DeBevoise 1986).

With the number and range of activities involving partnerships, all units in an institution increasingly are involved in efforts to support partnerships. For student affairs, partnerships with schools and businesses create opportunities for college readiness and transition programs, community service and student tutoring/mentoring programs, student internships and practicums, networks for exploring careers and career placement, and the involvement of educators and business people in enabling students to bridge the worlds of academe and business.

Summary

The responses to changing conditions employed by institutions have important implications for student affairs organizations. For student affairs professionals to be effective partners or leaders in strategic institutional responses, they will need to develop new and enhanced skills, programs, and services. Planning and management skills, including the employment of quality management, effective design and use of information technologies, the management of enrollments, raising funds from different sources, an understanding and application of cost containment, and skills needed to establish and foster partnerships, should be further developed. Student affairs professionals will be involved in planning and in program evaluation and research.

Most important in the development of new skills and programs is the realization that the combined talents of institutions will be needed to address changing conditions. Parallel but separate paths for faculty and student affairs professionals will no longer be tolerated in increasingly responsive and productive quality-oriented institutions.

The involvement in an increasing number of collaborative arrangements inside and outside the institution will reshape the traditional role of student affairs to a role that will be increasingly central to and integrated with institutional roles and priorities, a role that will move student affairs beyond the often isolated management of student life to a partnership with faculty and administrators concerned with the entire institution and its responses to changing conditions. Working as an environmental scanner, milieu manager, market analyst, legal adviser, development officer, researcher, and quality assurance specialist—as well as counselor, educator, and coordinator—the student affairs professional can be seen increasingly as one who seeks to integrate the goals of individual development with institutional development. To meet the demands of a new role, however, the student affairs professional must have a sound understanding of the role, the skills it requires, and the programs and services it demands.

Student affairs professionals will be involved in planning and in program evaluation and research.

THE INTEGRATOR: A New Role Explored

Since the late 1800s, faculty have transferred much of their responsibility for the social, affective, and moral development of students to student personnel professionals while retaining responsibility for the cognitive development of students. Likewise, the central mission of institutions—once both moral and academic—has become more purely academic, and, as a result, attention to the moral and affective development of students has been reduced to a supportive role. In this century, growing numbers of student affairs staff have assumed responsibility for students' extracurricular experiences, even as the student affairs function settled into a support role.

As the profession grew, it sought to define itself as distinctive within the higher education community. Engaging in this pursuit, however, might have unwittingly encouraged the belief that student affairs is a separate and less critical function than that performed by faculty. By establishing the affective domain as its province, student affairs positioned itself away from the intellectual heart of the institution. Today, observers still question whether student affairs is peripheral or central to an institution, and all too often, they reach the conclusion of 25 years ago—that it is peripheral (McConnell 1970).

Recognition is growing, however, that, in serving students, student affairs professionals are serving the institution in ways that are increasingly important to the institution's overall vitality and viability. That is, efforts to create inclusive campus environments, serve students' changing needs and interests, and bring principles of quality management to the campus are resulting in opportunities for leadership in student affairs, such as in recruiting and retaining students, fostering academic achievement, and contributing to the institution's efficiency. Furthermore, those efforts designed to *involve* students—on-campus employment, enhanced residential experiences, a variety of student activities—enhance the educational experience and contribute to the quality of education. Indeed, recognition is increasing that student affairs is a critical factor in promoting students' involvement (Astin 1985, 1992; Study Group 1984).

Participation in comprehensive efforts aimed at responding to changing conditions suggests a coordinating or integrative role for student affairs professionals. Student affairs is able to take the lead in formulating and implementing responses by integrating students' needs and traditional student affairs goals on the one hand and institutional goals and priorities on the other (Shaffer 1973; Silverman 1971, 1980; Wolfe 1993).

Assuming leadership by developing collaborative institutional responses to challenging conditions that benefit both students and institutions is a natural evolution of the student affairs function that places student affairs in a pivotal role within the institution.

To realize the potential of this role as integrator, student affairs professionals must be certain that their efforts are central to the institution's mission. To do so, student affairs professionals must move proactively to capitalize on the opportunities offered by changing conditions.

> *[By] anticipating the changes, trends, and developments [that] will affect higher education and the student populations, we can reconceptualize our approach to student services. . . . We must recognize that the need for many of the services we traditionally provided has been irrevocably changed or nullified by circumstances totally beyond our control and that our techniques for providing such services have, in many instances, been rendered obsolete by technological and managerial developments* (Brodzinski 1978, p. 5).

Student affairs professionals must assess their contributions to the institution and its students, work cooperatively with others in the institution to integrate those activities more completely with the institution's mission and goals, develop even greater expertise on students and their college experience, and become more active and creative in contributing that knowledge through comprehensive organizational responses to changing conditions (Dickson 1991). An "alert, assertive response to these forces [changing conditions] will make student affairs essential to institutional effectiveness" (Shaffer 1984, p. 112).

To capitalize meaningfully on this opportunity, student affairs organizations must engage in a variety of integrating actions, including developing an integrated mission within student affairs, integrating the theory and practice of student affairs, integrating the academic and student affairs communities, and integrating the campus and society.

Developing an Integrated Mission
Within Student Affairs

Student affairs professionals have by no means been exempt from the disagreement about the goals and purpose of higher education and the struggle associated with translating these perceptions to programs and services. "Over 215 different service or program titles [depict] the vast diversity of 'deeds' undertaken by members of the profession" (Hunter and Comey 1991, p. 10). Unfortunately, little has been accomplished in the last ten years in terms of clarifying, streamlining, or more consistently describing the roles that professionals assume.

Although several rationales for the existence and role of the student affairs profession have emerged over the years, they generally have been based in one of two primary perspectives: (1) a student-centered orientation with a focus on the personal needs and development of students; or (2) an institutional or administrative orientation with an emphasis on the management of programs, staff, and services (Delworth, Hanson and Associates 1989).

The perspective of *student developmentalist* is one in which the student is viewed primarily as a client whose personal development is the goal and direct product of the professional's efforts. Drawing on psychological theory and using techniques like counseling and psychoeducational interventions, the student developmentalist seeks ways to stimulate and support the student's psychological, intellectual, career, social, ethical, and cultural growth. The student affairs professional who employs an *administrative orientation* employs organizational and management theory in focusing his or her efforts most directly on enhancing the services, policies, and operations that make up the institutional infrastructure. The proponents of the administrative approach perceive themselves as working primarily for the institution and its goals and priorities.

A third philosophy, which integrates both administrative and student development orientations, is the *student services perspective*. This orientation not only incorporates elements drawn from each of the other two perspectives but also complements their endeavors. The student services orientation attends to the student in terms of his or her needs, which range from the basic concerns of life (shelter, food, safety, health) to those that support the academic mission (admis-

sions, academic skills, for example) to opportunities for affiliation (social or educational events, student clubs) to developmental services (counseling, testing, careers). Rather than seeking to exclusively promote the personal development of a particular student or the organizational development of the administrative infrastructure, however, the integrator assumes a role that facilitates the development of the whole student by creating, managing, and ensuring the availability of necessary institutional services and programs and a campus environment that serves both students and institutions.

A fourth integrative role for student affairs still has relevance for today's professionals (Crookston 1976). A manifesto for student development entitled "Student Personnel: All Hail and Farewell!" calls for professionals to recognize the limitations of both the terminology and the practice of student affairs exclusively as service management or "student personnel," as it was once commonly known, contending that the perceptions and role of student affairs professionals should be expanded to a more holistic conceptualization of the interaction between the student and his or her environment, that of *milieu management.*

> *What is milieu management? It is the systematic coordination and integration of the total campus environment . . . the organizations, the structures, the space, the functions, the people, and the relationships of each to all the others and to the whole . . . toward growth and development as a democratic community. In furtherance of human development theory, the relationships of the whole milieu with all its parts, and vice versa, must be symbiotic, or mutually enhancing or growth producing. Thus, as the individual and the group contribute to the total community, they give the community the capacity to create the conditions that contribute to the enhancement of the individual and the group* (Crookston 1975, p. 46).

Similar in concept to milieu management is the suggestion that student affairs professionals function as "campus ecology managers" (Banning 1989) and shift from viewing students as individuals to conceptualizing students as part of the larger campus interactive ecosystem.

Attending to students' and the institution's needs while managing the campus milieu enables student affairs professionals to recognize the interrelationship between students and institutional priorities and the need for proactive campus evolution. The milieu or ecology manager still needs to acquire expertise in student development and administrative development, but these individuals work within a larger, campuswide system context beyond those limited service areas traditionally viewed as the domain of student affairs.

The integration of the practices of student development and organizational development under the rubric of milieu management incorporates evolving trends in both areas. As theories of student development have evolved, they have increasingly begun to consider the critical shaping force of the various campus and off-campus factors on students (Huebner 1989; Baxter-Magolda 1992). Similarly, organizational theorists have come to realize how the changing nature of the student population, the explosion in technological innovations, the proliferation of litigation and legislation, shifts in the world political and economic structure, and the recognition of social problems on campus have affected the institution (Caple and Newton 1991). A marriage of these views provides the milieu manager with a special perspective on both student and organizational development. Recently, interest has been renewed in the notion that the student affairs profession must not view services, programs, or even students as mutually exclusive foci for its efforts (Bucci 1993). More important, it is in the facilitation of the interaction of these various components that the true function of student affairs exists.

As the unit with the most encompassing relationship with students and with other administrative and academic offices, the student affairs organization is the logical agency to assume the role of milieu manager on campus. Implicit in this rediscovered mission and role for the student affairs professional, however, is the need for student affairs professionals to possess a body of multidisciplinary knowledge and skills. Essentially, the milieu manager must be capable of designing and implementing interventions for students' development, the organization's development, and environmental development. Accordingly, he or she must be able to involve, teach, consult, advise, plan, budget, counsel, manage, research, evaluate, supervise, mediate, and train. If the student affairs profession is to rediscover, expand, and assume the comprehensive role of milieu management, then existing knowledge, skills, and perspectives must be expanded, and in some instances entirely new expertise must be acquired (Banning 1989; Frost 1991).

Integrating the Theory and Practice of Student Affairs

It is not unusual for the student affairs professional to become overwhelmed with the day-to-day supervision and management of an office or service. The omnipresent pressure of deadlines, accomplishing more with decreasing resources, legal liabilities, and responding to "political" forces causes the professional to put priorities on his or her efforts in ways that can diminish students' and the organization's development. As a practical reality, the pressures of daily responsibility override the importance of using developmental theory (Piper and Rodgers 1992).

While the concept of student development has received widespread support as the basis for the student affairs profession, the same cannot be said for organizational or administrative theories. Many student affairs professionals appear to be reluctant to fully incorporate organizational or administrative theory into their role. As a result of misunderstandings, administrative theory is frequently viewed pejoratively, while student development theory is embraced as the fundamental foundation for programs and practice (Vaala 1989).

That student affairs professionals have also exhibited a reluctance to strategically generate goals, design and implement programmatic interventions, and evaluate their effectiveness has seemingly been a function of conflicting priorities, the abstract nature of many theories, the difficulty in obtaining meaningful measurements, and a lack of training in translating theory to practice (Knefelkamp, Widick, and Parker 1978). But perhaps the most significant obstacle to the use of theory in practice is a pervasive attitude among student affairs administrators that although "interesting" to study in graduate school, theory is not something that one really uses in daily practice (Moore 1990). If student affairs professionals are to realize their full potential as integrators, they must understand, use, and apply theories—formal and informal, developmental and organizational—to design interventions and programs, effectively manage them, and modify them based on systematic evaluation.

Integrating the Academic and Student Affairs Communities

The distance, both literal and figurative, between student and academic affairs has undoubtedly fueled a great many mutual misconceptions about their respective roles and perspectives. Preliminary studies examining attitudes of student affairs staff and faculty have revealed that while both demonstrated an equivalent concern for students' development, neither constituency believed the other to be as concerned or capable of facilitating that outcome (Hintz and Stamatakos 1978). Such gaps are not unexpected, given the all-too-limited degree of interaction between academic and student affairs departments on most campuses. The failure of colleges to establish links between students' out-of-classroom experiences and their academic endeavors has impeded not only students' overall personal development but also the quality of their academic experience (Seldin and Associates 1990). Furthermore, this sometimes dysfunctional relationship has become one of the greatest sources of dynamic tension on the campus today (Boyer 1987). For institutions to meet students' needs more effectively, in and out of the classroom, and promote achievement, substantive communication between academic affairs and student affairs must increase.

Ironically, it is within the struggle to deal with some of the most difficult issues currently facing colleges that the greatest opportunities for such collaboration could exist. Certainly, the increasing diversity of the college population has been noted as a tremendous potential strength, but realizing that potential might not be accomplished without addressing the dilemma of balancing the desire for calm on campus and the inevitability of some degree of dissonance.

While the changing ethnic composition has been the most publicized aspect of diversity thus far, certain, perhaps less obvious, variations could present even more complicated challenges. Many of today's students are part of a generation that is not only ethnically diverse but also is culturally, economically, and in family structure diverse. Furthermore, it is the only generation born since the Civil War to come of age unlikely to match their parents' economic fortunes and the only one born in this century to grow up personifying not the advance but the decline of their society's greatness (Howe and Strauss 1993). The efforts of colleges to establish mean-

ingful multicultural communities have been impeded by esca-
lating campus violence, increased levels of observed psychopathology, and a prevailing attitude of cynical consumerism
from students who have been confronted by societal problems
that many faculty and administrators never encountered. Gain-
ing the respect and confidence of students who question a
professional's ability to understand their experiences is certainly not a new issue on campus, but motivating and preparing students who might feel disenfranchised to deal with
the complexity of interrelationships in today's global society
require an unparalleled unity between academic affairs and
student affairs. It can no longer be accomplished unilaterally
(Bricketto 1989).

Student affairs professionals, to the extent that they are
experts on students and enjoy a centralized position on campus, can be valuable resources for perplexed faculty, academic
administrators, and other staff who seek greater understanding
of today's diverse college population. Conversely, faculty support for student development goals is essential to their acceptance as institutional goals (Astin 1984). The weight of research demonstrating the positive effects of student affairs
professionals' efforts—shaped by student development theories—on students' satisfaction, persistence, and achievement
(Astin 1992; Pascarella and Terenzini 1991) establishes the
basis of students' development as an essential educational
goal. Yet:

> . . . *the suspicions and confrontations between faculty*
> *members and their institutions, nurtured by this absence*
> *of faculty from the total life of the institution, tears at the*
> *very fabric of a university, depriving it of the talent and*
> *energies so needed to accomplish its . . . mission* (Wood
> 1991, p. 3).

Clearly, collaboration between academic affairs and student
affairs is necessary to accomplish the goal of students' overall
development—both academic and personal. Therefore, creating opportunities for faculty and student affairs professionals
to share expertise is essential for an institution's viability and
vitality and features student affairs professionals as credible
experts within the institution.

Despite the potential power of this cooperative relationship between student affairs and academic affairs, overcoming a history of organizational segregation could continue to prove difficult. Many student affairs professionals have endured the notion of being on the periphery of the institution by claiming nonacademic development as their sovereign domain. The notion of now sharing that realm with faculty—even for the cause of advancing students' development—could prove to be threatening; that threat, however, must be viewed as an opportunity.

A realistic and practical integrated administrative approach is that of *functional teams management* (Jones 1988). This synergistic strategy is based on the notion that common situations, problems, and circumstances are interwoven in the interests and responsibilities of students, student affairs, and academic departments, and a functional team is assembled in relation to each common overlapping issue or area. A functional team designs coordinated strategies to diagnose and resolve only the particular common issue or area under consideration. One of the distinct advantages of this collaborative problem-solving approach is the potential for meaningful interaction among students, student affairs staff, and academic staff on many levels. Certainly, no shortage exists of identifiable common concerns that would provide the focal point for collaborative efforts between student affairs and academic affairs (see table 1).

Enrollment management can also present a logical and practical opportunity for collaborative partnerships between academic affairs and student affairs. First, attracting and retaining qualified students is in the best interests of all concerned campus constituencies, including students, faculty, administrators, and alumni. Second, in its broadest conceptual sense, enrollment management should be viewed as a process that extends well beyond admissions and directly involves strategies based on both academic affairs and student affairs to prevent the attrition of otherwise able students. Research studies investigating retention, persistence, and attrition have consistently concluded that, in conjunction with an individual student's characteristics, the ability of a student to academically and socially integrate into the institution is a critical factor in retention (Astin 1985). Helping students to make informed decisions about which college to attend, assisting them in the transition, and enabling them to be successful

Enrollment management can also present a logical and practical opportunity for collaborative partnerships between academic affairs and student affairs.

TABLE 1

POTENTIAL FOCAL POINTS FOR COLLABORATION BETWEEN ACADEMIC AFFAIRS AND STUDENT AFFAIRS

1. Help students to enhance ethical development by identifying and clarifying their academic, personal, career, and other values.

2. Manage disciplinary problems from a unified rather than a unilateral approach for consistency in response.

3. Reduce attrition and promote retention by addressing academic and nonacademic factors to manage enrollments.

4. Assess and evaluate services, interventions, and individual student development as part of research in student affairs.

5. Recruit and admit new students by addressing both academic and nonacademic factors in the selection process.

6. Enhance the freshman year to facilitate transitions and institutional integration.

7. Incorporate academic, avocational, and/or career interests with residential life programs.

8. Facilitate career decisions by recognizing the link between academic programs or courses and career choice.

9. Respond to alcohol and drugs on campus to prevent personal and academic debilitation.

10. Develop a holistic institutional mission with goals and objectives that incorporate cognitive, affective, career, physical, social, spiritual, and psychological development as interdependent features.

11. Respond to increased violence on campus.

12. Respond to increased psychopathology, balancing the needs of troubled students and the community.

in cognitive and affective growth are parts of an ongoing process that neither student affairs nor academic affairs is capable of accomplishing alone (Hossler 1985).

Working together, faculty and student affairs professionals can combine talents to better serve students and the institution. If one message has come from recent business literature, it is that discrete units serving their own self-defined interests cannot contribute effectively and efficiently to the organization's broader goals. Providing leadership to integrate efforts is a major opportunity for student affairs professionals.

Integrating Campus and Society

Higher education in the United States has an extensive legacy of preparing its graduates for roles as leaders of society—in business, government, religion, and an increasing array of professions (Carnegie Council 1980). Yet while responding to the evolving needs of society through research, teaching, and service, colleges frequently sought to insulate themselves from many of the very problems and issues they were preparing students to deal with (Harvey 1992). In truth, most colleges have a history generally of *reacting* to social changes rather than anticipating them and proactively intervening. Women, ethnic minorities, and students from lower socioeconomic classes, for instance, found their way into the academy more by default, legal stipulation, or economic necessity than by open invitation. Even today, many colleges are confused by increasingly diverse enrollments and how they might be changing the very nature of education.

Just as the campus is becoming more diverse, so too is the world community. We are witnessing movement from a collection of separate nations whose functions and fates were generally distinct to the development of a multinational economic society in which the interests of nations are inextricably interconnected. Currencies are common to all nations, trade barriers are being eliminated, and the problems of one nation have an inevitable impact on others. To reassert their positions as socially relevant and viable institutions, colleges will need to become proactive and to prepare students for this rapidly changing world, not just as it is but also as it will be.

It is for this new type of global society that we must seek to prepare leaders—those who can envision and understand how events in one part of the world will affect other areas. Unfortunately, many college students suffer from a profound lack of awareness of the significance of world and even local events and often have a feeling of being overwhelmed by the complexity of the world (Astin 1992). To assume responsibility for leadership in this new global society, student affairs professionals must learn to become facilitators and coordinators of efforts to help students develop a vision that extends beyond the campus gate and their personal aspirations.

Colleges can begin this process by helping their students learn about and become involved in local, state, and national issues. Although this idea was personified by the Freedom

Riders, Peace Corps members, and Vista volunteers of 30 years ago, such endeavors are receiving a renewed emphasis. In 1993, new legislation, growing out of grass-roots efforts by students and institutions and establishing a national initiative for community service programs for college students, was enacted with substantial financial aid incentives for participation in related programs. It will be incumbent upon colleges to design meaningful opportunities for such involvement.

Helping students to become aware of local, national, and world issues, to develop a sense of social responsibility, and to undertake practical experiences to enhance their expertise as leaders is a natural interdisciplinary role for student affairs professionals. Table 2 includes a number of suggestions that student affairs staff might institute to enhance their students' knowledge, skills, and values.

TABLE 2

POSSIBLE PROGRAMS TO INTEGRATE THE CAMPUS AND THE COMMUNITY

1. Offer campus programs to promote intercultural awareness and to enhance students' awareness of the many cultures and nations that make up the world community.

2. Develop community service programs to provide direct links between colleges and their communities.

3. Develop community service internships to provide students with hands-on intensive and regular opportunities to learn about and address real problems.

4. Develop campus programs that address real local and international issues rather than general, nonspecific topics.

5. Encourage students to become involved in their own campus community and with the organizations and problems that are part of that community.

6. Provide leadership training for students to develop their skills in addressing campus and community concerns through systems and organizations.

7. Develop the staff in terms of their awareness of local, campus, community, national, and international issues.

8. Encourage academic programs to include links, comparisons, and/or the perspectives of other cultures in the subject matter.

Summary

Student affairs professionals have a special perspective on institutions and their constituencies. Moreover, as the professionals who reach out to those who would be students and to those same students after college, they have a special understanding of the connectedness of the efforts of faculty, student affairs professionals, and the students themselves—and of all to the community and the world. Student affairs professionals must accept the challenge to use the talents of such experiences as integrators inside and outside the institution.

> *A number of forces and trends . . . are changing the nature and effectiveness of student affairs. The complex nature of the problems facing society is reflected in the problems of colleges and universities and amply demonstrates the difficulties of the profession. The challenge is not merely to work harder or longer but to perform duties and functions creatively and visibly so that there can be no institutional doubt as to the essential nature of student development oriented programs and services* (Shaffer 1984, p. 114).

To realize the potential of a role as integrator—to integrate students' needs, the goals of student affairs, and the institution's goals—calls for student affairs professionals to develop an integrated mission within student affairs, to integrate academics and student affairs communities, and to integrate the campus and society.

A shared vision of student affairs that is broad and inclusive is essential for its future. By integrating expertise in the theory and practice of students' development with that of organizational and administrative management in responding to changing conditions in society, the higher education enterprise, and among students, student affairs professionals can assume a more visible, viable, and vital role as leader in the institution.

CHALLENGES FOR THE STUDENT AFFAIRS PROFESSIONAL

The challenges for the student affairs professional in serving the institution in new roles are varied and demanding. Responding to students who are more diverse every year in ethnicity, age, career and avocational interests, and outlook is challenge enough. But as an integral part of organizations that are employing new strategies to respond to rapidly changing conditions, the role of student affairs is even more complex. Meeting these challenges requires student affairs professionals to use creative approaches. Managing student affairs is a whole new ball game (DeWitt 1991). Student affairs professionals who are responsible for coordinating institutional responses to changing conditions need to develop expertise in a multitude of areas—quality management, organizational and political skills, and research and evaluation—and integrate them with traditional skills.

In addition to developing, enhancing, and applying practical knowledge and skills, student affairs professionals serving as integrators must also be comfortable working with a variety of distinct theoretical perspectives and functional styles. They must be capable of blending together the respective contributions of many students, faculty members, and administrators to generate new models for collaborative leadership. Essential to enabling a role as integrative leader is for student affairs professionals to develop a clear vision, to become more effective and efficient decision makers, and to facilitate the development of creative and comprehensive strategies to address complex issues.

Developing Vision

Understanding and integrating students' and the institution's needs—needs that are constantly evolving—call for great skill. Given this need for student affairs professionals to constantly respond, adjust, and make transitions, they must have "broad knowledge, a sense of courage, a belief in a strong set of ethical and moral principles, and creative, imaginative minds capable of identifying many potentials" (Caple and Newton 1991, p. 112). In essence, the qualities necessary to be an effective college or university leader are not unlike those of the entrepreneur: seeing new markets or better ways of doing things, translating new concepts into clearly articulated goals, and, through others, bringing ideas to reality. An entrepreneurial leader has a vision—an ability to look ahead—without being trapped by what is happening at the moment. The visionary leader's awareness cannot be limited to the scope of activities within his or her office or department but must extend to the remainder of the institution and beyond the campus (Barr, Upcraft, and Associates 1990).

The visionary leader must also be able to conceptualize and clearly articulate a purpose and mission for the organization by incorporating the insights of colleagues. A shared vision enables new priorities, common goals, and joint responsibilities that will emerge and flourish not only in the form of programs and services but also as a sense of collaborative investment.

Unfortunately, under the press of daily obligations, student affairs professionals have either chosen or lapsed into the functional mode of day-to-day manager. Doing so, however, diminishes the future of student affairs, attention to students' needs, and the institution's ability to achieve its goals. Student affairs professionals must strive to be more than crisis managers if they are to be effective leaders.

The chief student affairs officer must function as an institutional leader in eight roles: articulator of a philosophy, advocate for students' needs and interests, transmitter of values, interpreter of institutional culture, institutional leader and policy maker, champion of causes, institutional planner, and public relations spokesperson (Stamatakos 1991). To serve in any or all of these roles calls for an encompassing vision that recognizes how the contributions of many individuals can be melded into real programs, services, and solutions.

While the ability to conceptualize a direction is an essential characteristic of leadership, the ability to translate this vision to organizational reality in the form of programs, services, staffing, and structures is a much more tangible administrative skill. The "art" of organizational change agentry has become an increasingly important element of college and university leadership, and student affairs professionals should look to a tactical approach to organizational change as a model for doing so (see, e.g., Creamer and Creamer 1991). As student affairs organizations struggle to respond to many emerging issues, innovative leadership and the ability to introduce and effect creative solutions will undoubtedly prove to be a key element of the student affairs professional's role.

Streamlining the Administrative Process:
Effective Decision Making

Student affairs organizations—embedded as they are in collegial institutions and consensus builders by nature—can also be viewed as indecisive (Barr 1988). Reliance upon collegiality as a means of making decisions and developing policy can become an expectation that can lead to an emphasis on process that minimizes concerns for outcome. In some instances, the practice of collegiality in planning and management might have been taken to such an extreme that it "gives the appearance that [student affairs professionals] are afraid to make a decision unless by committee" (DeWitt 1991, p. 187).

Such emphasis on process is an outgrowth of the role and voice of caretaker. Unfortunately, the hard issues of academic and institutional management—governance, curriculum, budgeting, management—can eclipse the issues voiced by student affairs. In fact, the voice of caretaker has typically been disregarded or overwhelmed by the voice of justice that dominates campus decision making (Hamrick and Carlisle 1990).

The strengths of active collaboration and communication, both within and between management components, are increasingly recognized as critical features of effective organizations (Barr 1993). Expeditious and unilateral decisions—once the hallmark of the strong manager—are increasingly contrary to principles of quality management. The challenge for student affairs professionals is to balance the strengths of a collaborative decision-making style with timely outcomes.

It is unlikely that many administrators individually possess the level of insight and expertise available through the collective input of a group of qualified staff members. While such active collaboration is essential for comprehensive planning and decision making, however, doing so is inherently a time-consuming process. Balancing the importance of soliciting colleagues' knowledge and skills is the need to foster each staff member's sense of personal investment in the situation, and the reality of the pressure to make timely decisions presents an imposing challenge for the student affairs professional who is seeking to function as an integrator: Ad hoc collaboration simply cannot be the vehicle for attempting to do so. Therefore, it is imperative that student affairs professionals design new types of administrative processes that are inclusive yet efficient (Porter 1989). Organized procedures must be developed for soliciting and organizing input—especially involving cooperation between student affairs and academic affairs—in the development of institutional goals, responses to daily problems, and the management of crises. Dependence on informal contacts, issue-driven ad hoc task forces, and other forms of reactive interactions must be replaced by organized strategies for proactive collaboration.

In that decisions are ultimately shaped by the quality of the information and the process available to administrators, an organized approach directly improves the quality of decisions. Student affairs professionals striving to become more effective decision makers must systematically assess, synthesize, implement, and evaluate. Intuitive understanding confirmed by anecdote is an insufficient basis for a student affairs program or organization. The limited capacity of many professionals to be able to clearly demonstrate their effectiveness is a glaring deficiency with professional and pragmatic implications (Bok 1986). Regardless of philosophical or operational perspective, student affairs professionals must be able to identify needs, design appropriate interventions, implement those interventions, measure outcomes, and evaluate the impact of programs and services. With more strategic information about programs and services, decisions can be more effective. Table 3 shows an organized collaborative decision-making and intervention planning model to improve decision making.

Developing Comprehensive Strategies
Beyond the need for student affairs professionals to develop an ever-wider array of expertise is the ability to integrate and apply this diverse knowledge and capability to real campus problems. Increasingly, comprehensive strategies are needed to address complex issues and concerns, such as dealing with troubled students, understanding and preventing attrition, and fostering a multicultural environment.

Responding to troubled students
Recent studies suggest that the number of students who manifest behavior associated with some form of a severe personal or psychological problem has dramatically increased (Gilbert 1992)—perhaps as much as tenfold (Gallagher 1989). Students who are struggling with academic, personal, or psychological problems might manifest this experience in the form

TABLE 3

A COLLABORATIVE ADMINISTRATIVE TAXONOMY

Phase 1: Collaboration. Establish a clear procedure for efficiently soliciting the input of campus faculty, administrators, and others with related information or expertise.

Phase 2: Presentation and Problem Identification. Assemble the collaborative team and/or implement the process for cooperative analysis. The initial goal is to clearly identify the problem and/or issue to be addressed with regard to the perspectives of academic affairs and student affairs as well as any other potentially related spheres, such as family, place of employment, membership on an athletic team or student organization, residence hall community, and so on. Involve representatives from each sphere determined to be relevant.

Phase 3: Information Gathering, Analysis, and Assessment. Through collaborative analysis, determine to what extent the issue involves discrepancies between ideal (mission) and actual levels of functioning in terms of:

1. *Student development:* The knowledge, skills, or level of personal development of individuals or groups of students. Which students are most critical, at risk, or in need?
2. *Organizational development:* The effectiveness and efficiency of policies, procedures, services, operations, or programs. Which organizational components are most critical, at risk, or in need?
3. *Environmental development:* The aggregate, social "press," or physical aspects of the campus environment. What aspects of the environment are most critical, at risk, or in need?

Phase 4: Identification of Goals and Objectives (Outcomes). Based on the comparison of the discrepancies found to exist between the ideals and the realities as identified during assessment as well as input from the collaborative process, identify specific outcomes that need to be facilitated in student development, organizational development, and environmental development as well as in other related spheres.

Phase 5: Collaborative Responsibility for Intervention. Given the identified goals and objectives for academic affairs and student affairs, and other spheres, determine the specific responsibility for developing related interventions.

Phase 6: Designing and Targeting the Intervention Strategy. Interventions (such as programs, organizational restructuring, classes, workshops, new facilities) should be designed to address the specific issues that were identified as concerns and appropriately targeted to those students, administrative components, or environmental fac-

TABLE 3 (continued)

A COLLABORATIVE ADMINISTRATIVE TAXONOMY

tors that are most critical, at risk, or in need. Determine a master timetable that establishes the date, time, location, and responsibility for each related intervention.

Phase 7: Consideration of Resources. Assemble the staff, money, facilities, equipment, and other resources to implement the interventions, and reassess your intervention strategies and/or goals if you do not have the needed resources. Rank the interventions in terms of perceived importance and available resources.

Phase 8: Evaluation. In the short term, how will you evaluate the extent to which each intervention strategy was effective? How will each outcome be measured in terms of the key variables to be examined and the evaluation process to be implemented? In the long term, how will you evaluate the extent to which the overall series and/or collection of intervention strategies made a difference on the campus? How will they be measured in terms of the key variables to be examined and the evaluation process to be implemented?

of impulsive behavior that is destructive to themselves or disruptive to others at school.

Student affairs staff frequently encounter situations in which a student's behavior, as a function of an underlying personal problem, calls for skills beyond those of the individual professional. In most instances, those professionals are expected to be able to identify a wide variety of problem behaviors and initiate appropriate referral—generally in the form of counseling or discipline. Even as increasingly complex problems are being observed on college campuses, however, legal, developmental, and ethical challenges are emerging associated with simply dismissing troubled students or providing short-term counseling.

The dismissal of students whose behavior creates chaos in the community is an understandable and sometimes necessary reaction (Brown and DeCoster 1989). Their presence can be disruptive on three distinct levels: the violation of campus policies, the taxing of campus crisis intervention services, and the concerns of friends and roommates whose limited exposure to such problems can draw them into codependent behaviors or cause them to react by fearing and withdrawing from the troubled individual. Despite the form of disruption, the indiscriminate use of punitive disciplinary sanctions or mandatory psychiatric dismissal as the primary means of dealing with these students can have ethical and legal consequences (Pavela 1985)—an opinion reinforced by the implementation of the Americans with Disabilities Act in 1992 (Frank and Wade 1993). Still, retaining such students leads to other dilemmas: To what extent should the college or university take active responsibility for students who are experiencing severe personal and/or psychological difficulties? Does the college have the responsibility or the capacity to function as a residential treatment center? And how does one balance the legal rights of the troubled student with the needs of others in the community?

While many institutions find they have little option other than dismissal, other institutions are attempting to generate campus-based alternatives for ongoing treatment of troubled students. Rutgers University, the University of Michigan, and New York University, for example, are among institutions that have designated specific residence hall areas as substance-free zones to provide a supportive haven for those students who are recovering from substance abuse or who would otherwise be troubled by even the presence of legal substances. Other collaborative strategies might include allowing the student to remain at the college under the conditions of reduced course loads, alternative residential arrangements, ongoing therapy, regular meetings with an adviser, or behavioral contracts.

The immediate dismissal of these students at the first sign of difficulty raises considerable moral and legal questions.

While the issue of the extent of institutional responsibility remains in question, the fact is that professionals will continue to encounter situations in which traditional disciplinary or counseling systems are inadequate. As levels of psychopathology increase on campuses, institutions might soon need to design more collaborative strategies to address the needs of psychologically troubled students whose presence can be mildly (not necessarily severely) "disturbing" to others (Delworth 1989). Many such students have the potential, with some degree of support, to complete college successfully. The immediate dismissal of these students at the first sign of difficulty raises considerable moral and legal questions.

College counseling centers, besieged by an influx of students seeking such assistance, are caught in the dilemma of quality versus quantity. For those students whose need is more one of support and validation, participation in group work has proven to be an effective alternative. A considerable number of students remain, however, who need more intensive psychotherapy. For many student affairs organizations, the only logical course of action has been to limit the number of allowable counseling center sessions and/or make immediate referrals to private off-campus agencies; indefinite psychotherapy sessions are no longer an option. While such a policy might be feasible at the urban or suburban institution with adequate community agencies, the same is generally not true for rural campuses. There, the decision to limit therapy could prove to have potentially dire consequences for the student-patient as well as for the other members of the college community (such as roommates and classmates) who might be directly affected by the impulsive behavior of a student who is struggling with an untreated psychological problem. More creative and expansive solutions are needed. As a guide, campuses should:

- *Develop comprehensive policies and procedures.* In conjunction with legal counsel, counseling center staff, and the disciplinary officer, the student affairs organization should first develop a clear policy on the circumstances and process through which a student can or will be suspended or expelled on psychiatric grounds. The Assessment-Intervention of Student Problems (AISP) model, for example, emphasizes distinguishing between psychiatric and behavioral factors (Delworth 1989). Because situations will arise when dismissal is the most appropriate response, having an established policy and procedure is imperative.
- *Integrate disciplinary and therapeutic responses.* Responses should include attention both to violations of behavior and to the psychological origin of the behavior. Unilateral counseling interventions could inadvertently send the student the message that his or her behavior was acceptable, and a disciplinary response without accompanying treatment could address the symptom while ignoring the cause of the behavior.
- *Collaborate with other professionals.* These matters involve decisions that have academic, psychological, and administrative implications. A case conference technique in which representatives from each unit operate as a campus intervention team by meeting to consider the incident,

meet with the student, make decisions, and develop cooperative responses is a critical component of the AISP model (Delworth 1989). As appropriate, the student's family might also become involved. With some modifications in each area, such as a reduced course load, a change in rooms, education of the roommate, counseling or treatment, and regular support from staff, the student's disruptive influence can be reduced and the potential to graduate increased.

Understanding and preventing attrition
Despite increased attention to managing enrollments, some projections suggest that over 50 percent of entering students will withdraw from the institution in which they enrolled before they obtain a degree (Giddan and Weiss 1990). The anticipated attrition rate for women and minority students is even more alarming (Levin and Levin 1991).

The extent to which a student has successfully been integrated, academically and socially, into the college environment appears to be significantly associated with the decision to remain at college (Astin 1985, 1992; Tinto 1987). Critical elements of persistence are the living environment, the classroom experience, academic advising, extracurricular involvement, financial support, and faculty involvement (Pascarella and Terenzini 1991). Clearly, the importance of one's peer group and the sense of being accepted as a member of the curricular and extracurricular groups of the college are of utmost importance (Stodt 1987a; Webb 1987).

The pervasive view of attrition and the related responses have tended to be institutional in nature. Administrators have sought to understand and address the causes on a global basis through efforts focused on identifying campuswide factors. A student does not form an immediate singular bond with the institution, however. An individual's decision to leave college occurs over time, shaped by the quality of interactions between that individual (and his or her own attributes, skills, and dispositions) and other members of the institutional academic and social systems (Tinto 1987). The contention is that neither integration nor attrition is a singular event but rather a progressive series of engagements, failures to engage, or disengagements with a multitude of academic and social elements on campus. Therefore, campus integration and involvement occur on many levels through the student's associations with multiple sub- or micro-environments, such as a residence hall group, formal clubs and organizations, an academic department, faculty, and informal campus peer groups. A student experiencing frustration or disillusionment in one micro-environment can still remain engaged and supported by his or her involvement in others. Conversely, disengagement from an institution might also occur in a similar manner. Eventually, if disengagement becomes too pronounced overall or if it occurs within an area of high priority for the student, attrition is likely.

Conceptualizing retention from this perspective can provide valuable insights in understanding the progressive nature of attrition. The early identification and response to students who are at risk could be a function of monitoring and facilitating their involvement, not merely in academic units but also in terms of each of the other micro-environments.

Through their roles in student life, student affairs professionals are in a special position to directly observe students integrating with or disengaging from campus environments. The extent to which a student becomes involved in the residence hall community, in clubs and other formal student organizations, fraternity or sorority life, athletic or intramural teams, and informal student groups should be readily apparent. Perhaps even more obvious is the student whose involvement is declining as he or she disengages from the group.

Student affairs professionals could be in a position to proactively enhance a student's respective skills to facilitate engagement in each area. Furthermore, through active involvement with students and the nonacademic aspects of the campus, student affairs professionals should be able to recognize the early stages of progressive disengagement and intervene immediately. The student affairs professional should examine attrition from the student organizations and communities with which he or she works and seek ways to prevent disengagement or encourage and facilitate the student's involvement with other campus groups. Failing to intervene until the student has already experienced repeated failures to integrate could prove to be too little, too late. In this manner, the student affairs professional becomes an integral component of a multifaceted institutional initiative to retain students (McIntire et al. 1992).

Developing a multicultural campus environment

Although representation still remains ethnically disproportionate, colleges and universities have already experienced
some significant transformations in their ethnic and gender
compositions. Unfortunately, as the enrollment of traditionally
underrepresented populations has increased, campuses have
not been free of the racism that erodes the capacity of the
campus culture to address the challenges and opportunities
of a more diverse student body. The challenge of creating a
diverse campus environment is undoubtedly one of the most
difficult issues that student affairs professionals will address
during the coming decade (Kalantzis and Cope 1992). A
limited understanding of intercultural issues and great urgency
to respond quickly hamper colleges' and universities' efforts.
Unfortunately, in the absence of clear goals and a thoughtful,
developmentally based plan as a foundation by which to
design and/or evaluate campus efforts, it remains difficult to
determine their efficacy. Despite their good intentions and
activities, leaders on many campuses have only begun the
task of moving the institution from a monocultural to a multicultural environment (Manning and Coleman-Boatwright
1991). Thus far, the prevailing imperatives for advancing
multiculturalism appear to include the demographic diversification of the student body, the creation of specialized student services, and the development of ethnic studies courses
(Wright 1987). A number of institutions have attempted to
introduce policies to regulate inappropriate and/or hostile
behavior, including speech that can be perceived as inciteful
or harassing, and most campuses have designed education
and awareness training programs, particularly within student
affairs organizations.

In terms of faculty and administrators, marginal advances
have been made in diversifying the student affairs professional
staff, but increasing the number of minority faculty has been
less successful (Sagaria and Johnsrud 1991).

*It is astonishing that more progress has not been achieved
in removing racism and clarifying the legitimate role of
minorities in university settings. . . . If higher education is
simply unable to progress, there may be more things wrong
within our still cloistered academic world than critics main-
tained in the 1960s. People change more slowly than insti-*

tutions, but evidence suggests that colleges and universities may be unable to change fast enough, at least in this arena (Siggelkow 1991, p. 100).

This limited success has led many to question whether the strategies colleges have employed have really effectively promoted an ethnically and culturally integrated campus. Social isolation and selective segregation are still readily apparent on our campuses. Many members of underrepresented groups who have not felt accepted by the dominant campus culture have chosen to affiliate primarily with one another for reasons of personal preference, a lack of feeling valued, and a pressure to conform to the standards and values of the dominant campus group.

Historically, the traditional method of dealing with a new campus population has been to assume that the campus melting pot would encourage these new students to adopt the majority's values. Today, that perspective has been modified with an increased focus on identifying and promoting commonalities among students rather than emphasizing differences. Yet within this positive approach still exists the tacit assumption of some sort of monocultural campus community as the ideal goal. Doing so could be a failure to recognize the importance of ethnic and cultural identity to individual students. That differences exist is not inherently a negative: Learning to appreciate and value those differences is the key. From the perspective of student development, learning about others is a function of interaction and exposure. When our perceptions of one another are based on stereotypes, media images, and fears, a certain degree of dissonance is to be expected when we come together—whether on or off campus. The challenge is to acknowledge, manage, and transform that dissonance into meaningful development. Efforts by administrators to devalue differences, avoid uncomfortable discussions, and prevent conflicts are understandable; however, such actions can unintentionally also constrict not only individual development but also the emergence of an honest campus environment where misunderstandings and apprehensions can be openly addressed and resolved. Student affairs professionals must help institutions find a balance between calm on the campus and productive dissonance.

Seeking to create a multicultural or culturally pluralistic campus environment, student affairs professionals must simultaneously address the needs and interests of a variety of student groups, striving for their respective cultures to be recognized on campus. Efforts to accomplish these goals have all too often precipitated negative or cynical reactions from members of the dominant student population, who fear what they see as the potential erosion of their own culture.

Establishing a multicultural campus environment is an evolving process, and if the transition is to be successful, educators must do more than recruit a significant number of diverse students and then respond to any related problems as they emerge. They must search for ways to conceptualize and address multiculturalism proactively from three perspectives: student development, organizational development, and environmental development (see table 4).

The process of inclusion for members of underrepresented groups involves seven critical elements: adequate financial aid programs, an environment that supports multiculturalism, academic retention programs, faculty involvement, communication with prospective students and their high schools, a social climate that instills a sense of comfort, and commitment by the institution's leaders (Brown 1991). These objectives cannot be accomplished through unilateral interventions and segregated services. While students are being urged toward mutual appreciation of cultural differences, student affairs and academic affairs staffs cannot continue to work in isolation. The traditions of academia are strong, and for the many faculty, administrators, and staff whose own college experiences were at a predominantly monocultural campus, their personal and professional growth will be a necessary precursor to establishing an environment that not only protects the basic rights of each campus cultural group, but also seeks to encourage expression (Hossler 1985).

Summary
The nature and scope of problems that have become critical concerns for the student affairs professional vary by institution, and this discussion is not intended by any means to be exhaustive. Given the demographic and cultural changes in students, economic trends that have imposed greater fiscal restraints on colleges, legal decisions and actions that demand compliance, social issues and problems that confront and influence students, and political and administrative institutional forces, the role of the student affairs professional could

TABLE 4

CRITICAL PHASES IN DEVELOPING
A MULTICULTURAL CAMPUS

1. Establish clear definitions and realistic goals.

2. Establish a comprehensive plan, including student development, organizational development, and environmental development.

3. Prepare and involve the campus and community.

4. Develop the current staff's expertise on multiculturalism, and hire minority staff.

5. Develop support services and programs for minority students, and enhance intercultural expertise of existing services.

6. Establish related behavioral policies and standards to deal with inappropriate behavior.

7. Encourage the involvement of student organizations in increasing membership of minorities.

8. Offer a variety of educational and social intercultural programs.

9. Incorporate minority perspectives in academic courses.

10. Develop and educate minority students to prepare them to deal with the transition to campus and to facilitate integration and involvement.

11. Develop and educate majority students to encourage intercultural awareness.

12. Establish a mentor group program for minority students to provide ongoing support.

13. Encourage minority students to assume positions of leadership on campus.

14. Recognize innovations and efforts of individuals and departments in facilitating multiculturalism.

15. Evaluate progress toward meeting the goals.

be more stressful than ever before. As a result, student affairs professionals, to better serve students and their institutions, must be prepared to develop an enhanced vision, become more efficient and effective decision makers, and lead efforts to develop comprehensive strategies.

CHALLENGES FOR STUDENT DEVELOPMENT:
The Need for Focus and Research

Formal and informal notions of student development have shaped college experiences since colonial times. During the 1960s and 1970s, however, the emergence of specific models that sought to explain the content and process of development prompted many to view this perspective as a logical unifying theoretical or operational foundation for student affairs. Student affairs professionals must understand and seek to integrate a variety of developmental theories and models, effectively translate theory into practice, and advocate for or engage in research on student development.

Employing student development as a unifying theoretical or operational foundation for the profession is difficult. First, despite some general commonalities, the variety of student development theories often employ different terminology, present distinct notions of what constitutes development, and offer different or minimally defined outcomes. Therefore, no single accepted standard or conceptual framework of student development exists upon which practitioners can base the design of interventions and measure their success.

Second, translating student development theories into effective practice has often been elusive, because many theories are complex and difficult to translate. And for many student affairs professionals, daily pressures preclude planning and reflecting on theories in the design and delivery of programs and services.

Third, the college population has radically changed since student development theories were originally devised. Theories based on the predominance of white males between the ages of 17 and 22 have proven to be inadequate in considering the developmental process of women, nontraditional students, members of varying ethnic and cultural populations, and those whose sexual orientation is homosexual (Moore 1990).

Fourth, many student development theories are predicated on a more or less closed campus environment. Today, with campuses reaching out and students balancing a number of different roles, a broader understanding is needed of how students develop and the shaping effects of their many contexts.

Fifth, integrating efforts to promote student development with administrative practices continues to be challenging. And, sixth, the paucity of a meaningful research base to validate existing theories has limited their applicability. The student

For many student affairs professionals, daily pressures preclude planning and reflecting on theories in the design and delivery of programs and services.

affairs professional needs a focus for and substantive research on the utility and practice of student development.

The Evolution of Student Development

In a general sense, student development is the application of the principles of human growth in the context of higher education. While perhaps not formally recognized as such, elements of student development have always been inherent in the relationship between students and a college or university. Even the responsibilities of moral development and the notion of acting in loco parentis were basic manifestations of a set of beliefs about the nature of students and their needs for growth and guidance (Moore 1990). But it was not until the latter part of the 19th century that William Rainey Harper, president of the University of Chicago, was moved to call for the "scientific study of the student" and the formal incorporation of the principles of psychology in higher education (Herr and Cramer 1979). Shortly thereafter, three distinct movements began to emerge that would eventually come together to give birth to student development as a focus for colleges and universities.

First, the notion that one's experiences as a child and adolescent shaped adult life was promoted through the wide popularization of Freudian concepts of human development near the end of the 19th century. This adoption of psychological principles of personal growth eventually led to the sweeping mental hygiene movement of the early 1900s.

Second, the burgeoning industrialization of the United States created a great need for helping individuals learn about and choose a vocation that would be a good fit with personal skills, needs, and interests. Essentially a merger of these new psychological concepts of personality and other characteristics with vocational selection, career testing and guidance became pronounced functions in the years after World War I. Educational institutions were urged to establish curricula that encouraged students to integrate their values, education, and life-style by linking their beliefs with their career.

Third, student affairs struggled to establish a clear professional identity and purpose, and it was in the movement toward vocational guidance that many student affairs staff saw a clear parallel role on their own campuses. The personnel guidance movement, by combining the tenets of psychology with the process of vocational testing and counseling, afforded a clear opportunity for student affairs to assume a vital role in higher education. In the years between the end of World War I and the depression of the 1930s, that promise was fulfilled to an unprecedented, and perhaps since unequaled, extent (Fenske 1989).

This new role was described and embraced in a 1937 statement by the American Council on Education, which served as a clarion call for student affairs to be concerned with the education and development of the whole student as a philosophical basis for the profession—the foreshadowing of the perspective of student development.

During the subsequent three decades, various theorists gained and lost favor as student affairs professionals struggled to understand the elusive concept of the whole student (Wrenn 1968). In fact, little common agreement existed as to what constituted development, how this process actually occurred, or the extent to which growth could and should be intentionally facilitated.

While the debate continued, the tumultuous 1960s provided even greater impetus for practitioners to clarify how college students developed. Theorists, such as Nevit Sanford, Arthur Chickering, William Perry, and Lawrence Kohlberg, developed models that focused on the internal process of growth and development. Others, such as Theodore Newcomb and Kenneth Feldman, contended that the secret to the developmental process was in the study of the environment. They and many other subsequent researchers investigated how the characteristics of the institution serve as factors in enhancing or inhibiting students' personal development.

The acknowledgment that differences in development could be only partially explained by institutional differences was underscored by the growing diversity of the campus population. Recognition grew that individual and cultural differences and characteristics might have been overlooked as significant factors in development (Astin 1977; Tinto 1987). As a result, student development professionals have been urged to concentrate on developing and targeting interventions for specific groups of students rather than for the entire student body. The use of general universal theories has given way to more focused models that consider the special experiences of each student group.

But the enthusiasm over the preliminary findings of student development has dimmed (Brown and Barr 1990). Too many generalizations have resulted in misapplication, and the idealism of what initially seemed to be a powerful tool for guiding and shaping student affairs is being replaced by the realization that rethinking and considerable hard work remain.

Today, the term "student development" has evolved into a generic means of referring to four distinct, but related elements. It is used interchangeably to refer to (1) the process of growth and change, (2) the outcome of growth and change, (3) the intervention strategies intended to facilitate growth and change, and (4) the set of administrative offices and services charged with the responsibility for delivering developmental programs (Miller and Winston 1991). Further complicating communication among professionals is the fact that student affairs professionals come from a variety of backgrounds with different education and experiences. The absence of a singular agreed-upon definition for student development has led to differing translations and, hence, variations in knowledge, skills, and perspectives among professionals.

Translating Theory into Practice: The Process Model
The failure of theories of student development to clearly detail the process by which growth actually takes place has limited their practical utility. Having an understanding of stages, positions, or phases of development can provide a student affairs professional with a means of approaching a student and offering an idealized direction for future development, but many theories often neglect or only superficially address the process by which students actually undergo such growth.

For every student, a distinct set of issues, experiences, and other forces collectively exerts a shaping force on that student's attitudes, knowledge, identity, and behavior (Oetting 1967). As a result, it is unusual for two students to respond to the same stimulus in quite the same way. Given the inadequacy of any one individual theory in addressing these issues, some suggest that it is only through the use of a battery of theories and an emphasis on the process of development that the practitioner can effectively meet the needs of diverse students (Andreas and Krager 1989).

Despite the complexity of development, student affairs professionals facing the daunting task of attempting to facilitate a student's growth have found the use of pragmatic informal approaches to be a viable alternative (Rodgers 1991). Logical notions of "how things happen" integrated with more formal and researched conceptualizations have proven to be useful and infinitely more communicable approaches to student development (Rhatigan 1975).

The developmental process models provide a systematic format for translating a theory to intervention. A well-known example, the Council of Student Personnel Associations (COSPA) model, provides a ten-step approach to putting theory into operation. Such models serve to transcend differences among formal theories by providing a step-by-step account of the process of development and affording the student affairs professional with a realistic framework for putting a theory into operation.

New Populations, Old Assumptions

In countless works, student affairs professionals have been urged to recognize that the population of the United States is changing significantly. This diversity has come to be reflected more slowly on college campuses. The white, middle-class, 17- to 22-year-old male cohort that has dominated the college population has been replaced by a much more varied student body.

With new student clienteles has come a change in perspectives on student development. Theories and models that emerged during the 1960s and 1970s have been subjected to a great deal of scrutiny. Of primary concern is the manner in which many of these theories were developed, particularly the use of the then much more homogeneous student population as a means of formulating central hypotheses. Efforts to now extend and apply these theories to today's radically different student body have been met with much criticism (Moore 1990). Research conducted during the 1980s confirmed the significance of individual and cultural characteristics as critical factors in development, especially those that serve to differentiate one from the majority population in a given environment (Schlossberg, Lynch, and Chickering 1989). It is now understood that many student development models were potentially ethnocentric, sexist, and culturally biased in origin. They tend to define development according to the standards of the population that dominated the environment when they were formulated. By failing to consider the importance of cultural differences and priorities and by pronouncing any variations from the model norms as being deviations and/or developmental deficiencies, a great many of these early models must be revised (as Chickering has done) or disregarded in working with diverse student populations.

Student affairs professionals are realizing that neither the use of a single developmental model nor the implementation of mass intervention strategies is as effective as matching the model and intervention with the student or student subgroup. Thus, the professional employing a developmental approach must become conversant with a cluster of discrete theories and understand their differences and similarities. Separate models explain the developmental process from an ethnic, gender, age, cultural, and sexual orientation point of view. The task of the student affairs professional is to be familiar with a variety of models, recognize the nature of individual students and student groups, and apply an appropriate model in an individualized manner (Brown and Barr 1990).

The Expanding Environmental Context

The limitations of student development theories extend beyond cultural and individual differences to the effects of campus and community environments. Early theories considered the context of the small closed campus environment, one that rarely exists today. Significant changes in communication, transportation, and economic interdependence have made our world a global village and the campus an active, if reluctant, participant. Students bring with them and continue to be subjected to the influences of those forces and events that exist or occur well beyond the gates of the college (Kuh 1981a).

The college is no longer the only environmental context within which the student functions. Rather, it is only one aspect of the student's life and but one source of influence on him or her. Developmentalists have come to realize that human growth is a complex process in which the individual's special cognitive, affective, and behavioral characteristics are modified through exposure to and interaction with all of the messages, people, and experiences with which or whom the person comes in contact.

Unfortunately, many theories of student development fail to present adequate explanations as to how the environment directly or indirectly shapes cognitive and affective development. Of the 24 theories practitioners use most, only four strongly emphasize the quality or nature of the environment in promoting development (Rodgers 1991). Of the person-environment theories, a question exists as to whether they are so complex that they defy effective implementation (Huebner and Lawson 1990). The student affairs professional, however, cannot ignore or underestimate the respective influence of the many on- and off-campus variables that simultaneously affect a student.

Emerging alternatives to the psychosocial, cognitive, and person-environment development models that have so far dominated the profession are college impact models. Impact models emphasize the interaction between the student and the environment (Astin 1985; Pascarella 1985; Tinto 1987). In considering the extent to which a student has become personally engaged and invested in various segments of the campus community—generally termed degree of involvement or integration—impact models allow the practitioner to examine and understand how these campus interactions influence the individual's development.

Impact models consider the significance of institutional policies, programs, and services as well as the effect of formal and informal campus groups, and the somewhat more conceptual environmental factors like aggregate values, norms, and behaviors on the student (Pascarella and Terenzini 1991). Furthermore, these models also address the impact of differences within and between institutions and the influence of noncampus variables to a much greater extent than their predecessors (Weidman 1989).

Integration with Administrative Practice
Perhaps the clearest challenge for student development theory is its integration with administrative practice in colleges and universities. Student development theory implies the development of students as the guiding principle for student affairs organizations, but these organizations are also units of institutions that have related but different goals and priorities. In formulating responses to changing conditions, student affairs organizations must attend to both students' and institutions' needs; they must respond to students and systems. If student affairs professionals succeed as integrators, then they must attempt to foster the institution's or the organization's development as well as students' development (Borland 1980).

To the extent that the profession has become focused on students' development and neglected institutional goals, it has risked becoming more peripheral. Others in the institution have rarely embraced student development practices. The goals of institutions and student affairs are often not integrated, and student development has not been incorporated into administrative or academic practice.

Concerns about finances and enrollments argue for undertaking preservation of the institution; despite an increasing recognition of the importance of nonacademic factors, however, student affairs is rarely perceived as the primary or leading provider of services that could lead to students' retention (Green 1983; McIntire et al. 1992). Such is the case until and if student affairs professionals offer a convincing argument for the importance of students' development to the institution and to students. Failing to do so threatens the future of student affairs. Simply put, student development must become more institutional and the institution must become more oriented toward students' development if both are to flourish.

The Need for Research
Understanding and applying the development of students effectively depends on substantial research.

> *Student affairs staffs are expected to be experts on students and campus environments. . . . If what is published in student affairs and higher education journals accurately reflects what is known about the undergraduate experience, clearly student affairs staff must learn a good deal more about what actually takes place on their campuses* (Kuh and Andreas 1991, p. 397).

The inability to clearly and conclusively demonstrate the connection among variables like campus characteristics or intervention programs and student outcomes is a severe handicap for the student affairs professional. Without the availability of a strategic research base, practitioners on many campuses are forced to rely on the smorgasbord method in which a great many general programs are offered on campus with the hope that the students who most need assistance will decide to help themselves by attending or somehow unavoidably stumble upon the programs if enough are presented. Certainly, the availability of social and educational opportunities is important, but the ability to ascertain whether separate or collective interventions in students' development accomplish their intended goals is crucial. If student affairs professionals are to translate theories of student development into practice, they must know why and how a practice works, not just *that* it works, and be able to validate that knowledge by applying it to other students and in other situations (Lenning 1989).

Research on student development can be categorized in three distinct areas:

1. Sociological research that explores the relationships between students in general and the environment in which these students exist.
2. Psychological research that investigates the manner in which an individual student progresses along a given theoretical continuum.
3. Outcomes research that seeks to understand the impact of college attendance upon nontheoretical variables like persistence, satisfaction, socioeconomic status, and life-style (Stage 1989).

Unfortunately, the existing research is generally considered insubstantial both in form and content, limiting one's ability to draw upon other than tentative conclusions about relationships among and between variables (Pascarella and Terenzini 1991). Another significant concern is the realization that there could be few, if any, actual singular direct relationships between one independent variable and a particular outcome. Researchers have begun to conceptualize outcomes as the result of the combined interactive effects of numerous variables that affect one another and only eventually are indirectly and relatively linked with a given outcome (Stage 1989). Because development is an individualized process, however, researchers are as yet unable to predict outcomes with assurance.

Although faculty and other independent researchers have made many significant contributions, substantive research by student affairs practitioners has been rare (Johnson and Steele 1984). Most studies done by practitioners have relied on data obtained from survey research and/or qualitative techniques like focus group interviews to guide administrative decision making and interventions in students' development (Malaney and Weitzer 1993). Certainly, surveys and qualitative research are of immense practical value in identifying and understanding the issues facing students, the extent to which particular problems or characteristics are prevalent on a campus, and factors associated with students' and the organization's development. It is also necessary, however, to conduct subsequent research to determine the impact of interventions and to discover whether what is being done really makes a difference.

While the body of independent research to refine theories of student development and test the techniques used to make them operational has been growing, the challenge remains to encourage campus practitioners not only to use these findings but also to conduct their own investigations to provide a foundation, direction, and validation of their own efforts (Astin 1990). The challenges of conducting research in a field setting can be overwhelming, yet the need for meaningful data to guide programs and interventions is critical. A review of research by student affairs practitioners makes several basic recommendations to promote additional meaningful practical research in the profession:

1. Researchers must develop well-designed, valid, and reliable instruments to measure the constructs associated with student development.
2. Investigators should provide journals to record information about reliability, validity, format of items, number of items, scoring procedures, and normative data, and a test manual with the instruments used in their research projects.
3. Normative data pools should be developed for each major construct and made available to researchers and practitioners.
4. Researchers need to clearly link theories of student development to their research to test and affirm or disprove those theories.
5. Researchers need to extend their studies to new populations that have previously not been included in investigations to broaden the scope of the research base.
6. Commission IX of the American College Personnel Association should be given greater visibility and ability to make unpublished instruments more available to practitioners (Tinsley and Irelan 1989, p. 446).

A recent review of research in student affairs suggests that cost and expertise are critical factors in the extent to which a student affairs organization engages in meaningful investigation and presents an overview of 15 specific research methods available to practitioners based on these two concerns (Malaney and Weitzer 1993). Student affairs organizations should make a commitment to a research agenda as a priority in students' development, for "student affairs professionals who learn to use research in support of their planning, policies, and decisions will be the best equipped to advocate for student affairs in the coming years" (p. 136).

Summary: Recommitting to Student Development

Since the term "student development" was coined almost 30 years ago, the search for a universally accepted definition with standardized outcomes and measures continues. If the potential of student development as a theoretical, philosophical, and operational foundation for the profession is to be fully realized, however, fundamental challenges must first be resolved. Student affairs professionals, in their role as integrators, must recommit themselves to student development and tackle the challenges of diverse theories and models, theoretical limitations, and integration with administrative practice. The price for failing to do so will be ongoing confusion and inconsistency and limited recognition of the significance of student development in the educational process. It could ultimately be the ability of student affairs practitioners to demonstrate their effectiveness as student developmentalists that could be the most critical aspect of attaining professional recognition and serving as institutional leaders.

Yet even within the student affairs profession itself is disagreement over the equality of student development and academic achievement as elements of the mission of higher education. In fact, one section of the 1987 *Perspective on Student Affairs* written to commemorate the 50th anniversary of the publication of the *Student Personnel Point of View* defines the role of student affairs as secondary to the academic mission and urges student affairs to continue to assume a supportive role (Baxter-Magolda 1992). But as colleges and universities face the 21st century, student affairs professionals must strive for greater awareness of the process of growth and the nature of the changes that they know college students will experience. Understanding the true impact of college and intentional efforts to promote student development and achievement is critical to student affairs professionals' assuming new, more central roles in institutions.

Even within the student affairs profession itself is disagreement over the equality of student development and academic achievement.

PREPARING STUDENT AFFAIRS PROFESSIONALS FOR CHANGING ROLES

Changes in students' and institutions' natures and needs consistently prompted an evolution in the role of student affairs
as colleges struggled to redefine their relationship with students (Allen and Garb 1993). To be a viable profession, however, student affairs must take the lead in defining its future
in the academy. Student affairs professionals must have a
sense of the changes in the field and of the influential factors
emerging from other sources that prompt its continuing evolution. For student affairs professionals to function as integrators, they must have strong interpersonal and organizational skills, including planning and budgeting, management
and supervision, and research and evaluation.

Initial preparation in the student affairs profession should
strive to prepare individuals to be effective in both students'
and organizations' development. No graduate preparation program, however, regardless of profession, can provide graduates with all the skills and knowledge needed to sustain a
vital professional life. Changing needs and conditions, new
opportunities and challenges, emerging theories, and new
research findings cause professions—and the skills needed
to practice them—to evolve continually. Providing student
affairs professionals with broad attention to the skills needed
to formulate effective responses to changing conditions
should be an ongoing goal of graduate programs and of institutional and individual professional development plans.

Graduate Preparation Programs
Defining the skills and experience necessary for entry into
the field is difficult in student affairs for many reasons. First,
the variety of roles in which student affairs professionals serve
makes it difficult to define the common core of knowledge
and skills (Hunter and Comey 1991). Second, individuals
enter the profession in a variety of ways, and it is not unusual
for many student affairs professionals to receive little or no
graduate training in the field. Many student affairs professionals enter the field almost by accident, often making a decision
near the end of their undergraduate education because of a
critical experience or the encouragement of an influential person (Hunter 1992). Third, the diversity in preparation, outlook, and approach continues to be a source of both strength
and weakness for the profession, continually feeding the
debate about whether student affairs constitutes a profession

under any definitions of the term (Stamatakos and Rodgers 1984).

In fact, graduate preparation programs tend to vary greatly in philosophy, content, and departmental location (Keim 1991). A study of graduate degree programs for student affairs professionals found that about 36 percent are oriented toward counseling, 29 percent emphasize administration, 25 percent focus on general human development, and 10 percent have no particular concentration (Rodgers 1983). Variety in the type of preparation received by graduate students has made many administrators wary, questioning whether new professionals are adequately prepared to carry out the variety of responsibilities particular to entry-level jobs or have the potential for leadership and depth of understanding necessary for upward mobility (Ebbers and Kruempel 1992). Many contend that the problem of professional credibility and acceptance is compounded by the lack of consistency in curricula for preparation programs and by the methods used in the education of future student affairs administrators (Beatty and Stamatakos 1990).

Despite attempts to establish a common core for preparation of student affairs professionals, such common learning is elusive (Hunter and Comey 1991). Recently, the Council for the Advancement of Standards (CAS) developed and promoted guidelines for preparation (Miller and Winston 1991) that designate three distinct major areas: student development, administration, and counseling. Each area contains sets of prescribed coursework and practical experiences that promote competence (Ebbers and Kruempel 1992). These standards hold great promise for the profession as a common core to help define itself while retaining the flexibility of programs to develop specific strengths. A number of leading graduate preparation programs have embraced the guidelines in the design of their programs. The CAS guidelines are voluntary, however, and it could be some time before it can be determined whether they successfully establish a common core for the profession.

Another method to ensure comparability in the preparation of student affairs professionals is the notion of providing credentials or certifying professionals. Such a process could afford student affairs a means of distinguishing those who possess appropriate professional training from those who do not (Mable and Miller 1991). Certification includes two central elements: successful completion of a graduate program in student affairs that conforms to the standards presented by the CAS standards or a similar model, and satisfactory achievement on a variety of assessments, including tests of general and specialized knowledge and demonstration of effective professional practice. Attempting to develop and have accepted a process of certification would undoubtedly be controversial, but it could provide some unity within the profession and provide an opportunity to establish definitive entry-level requirements for knowledge, skills, and dispositions.

An integrative curriculum

Most graduate preparation programs require the student to accumulate a specified number of credits in coursework, often with a particular emphasis in administration, counseling, or student development (Rodgers 1983). Many graduate programs, even those conforming to the CAS standards, typically offer a quasi-counseling or a quasi-administrative degree (Delworth, Hanson, and Associates 1989). Regardless of concentration, programs must address the knowledge and skills necessary for student affairs professionals to meet the challenges of changing conditions and to work effectively with both students and the institution. Put simply, for a student affairs professional to be effective at promoting the development of students, he or she must understand how to engage in organizational decision making that can facilitate that goal; likewise, the effective administrator must be able to understand and apply student development theory to design and deliver programs effectively. Employing a specific set of interdisciplinary knowledge and skills to design and implement student development, organizational development, and environmental development interventions, the broadly prepared student affairs professional brings special talents to an institution.

A proposal for graduate preparation that departed significantly from previous models in recognizing the variety of skills necessary to be a successful student affairs professional in a changing world contends that student affairs work is conducted in an interactive, institutional context (Brown 1985). To accomplish the goals of student development, one must understand how this system developed, functions, and affects those who inhabit it. As such, it is congruent with the role of integrator or milieu manager.

Using this model (Brown 1985) as a foundation, the model in table 5 is presented as a means of identifying specific areas in which graduate programs should offer training. No attempt is made to delineate precisely how many courses a student should take in each area or to identify alternative means by which development in each might be fostered. Rather, it assumes that graduates should develop competence in each area. Table 5 reflects a student affairs graduate curriculum that, when integrated, should facilitate a comprehensive sense of professional expertise.

Enhancing continuing professional development

Despite the efforts of student affairs preparation programs to prepare new professionals to serve in a wide variety of roles, continuing professional development is necessary to maintain and enhance skills, develop new knowledge and skills, and develop effective, collaborative responses to changing conditions. The realities of day-to-day pressures on time and money often make it difficult for student affairs organizations or professionals to engage in an effective program of professional development. A substantial relationship exists between professional development and the effectiveness of student affairs organizations and the institutions of which they are a part (Creamer and Shelton 1988).

The continuing needs for professional development of novices and experienced professionals are somewhat different. New professionals require effective orientation to the institution and induction into the profession. More experienced staff need opportunities for enhancing their professional vitality. And both novices and experienced professionals need continuing involvement in opportunities to enhance their knowledge and skills.

Orienting and inducting new professionals. Employers of new student affairs professionals must recognize a responsibility to provide new staff with ongoing training and support to build expertise, develop professionalism, and provide opportunities to evaluate and improve performance. Given the variety of training and experience of newly hired student affairs professionals, efforts should be undertaken to build the skills of new professionals in the areas outlined in the proposed model for graduate preparation.

In addition, the seven of 45 skills deemed to be most critical are leadership, student contact, communication, personnel

TABLE 5

PROFESSIONAL PREPARATION PROGRAM MODEL FOR STUDENT AFFAIRS PROFESSIONALS

Program Aspect	Student-Oriented Expertise	Organization-/Institution-Oriented Expertise
Understanding the Collegiate Experience	The College Student Cultural Diversity	History/Philosophy of Higher Education History/Philosophy of Student Affairs Current Issues in Higher Education
Understanding Theory	Learning Theory Developmental Theory Counseling Theory	Organizational Theory Management Theory
	Person-Environment Interaction Theory	
Developing Competence	Counseling Practices Instructional Strategies Intervention Strategies	Planning and Budgeting Management and Supervision Program Assessment and Evaluation Research Design Law and Higher Education
Developing General Practical Skills	Conflict Mediation Presentation of Workshops	Written Communication Skills Time Management Skills Technical Innovation Skills
Professional Practice	Counseling Practicum	Internship
Developing Professional Standards	Professional Ethics Professional Standards Legal Standards Professional Activities and Involvement Professional Philosophy	

management, fiscal management, professional development, and research and evaluation (Gordon, Strode, and Mann 1993). Assessment of a new professional's skills and knowledge in each area should form the core of the orientation and professional induction agenda upon initial appointment. Efforts should then be made to build the competencies of all professionals to a comparable level while allowing for specialization.

Other features of a professional orientation and induction plan should focus on developing an individual's understanding of the institution's mission and goals, philosophy of student affairs, priorities for institutional affairs and student affairs, and general information about the institution's current status and future plans. In addition, all new professionals must understand the philosophical orientation and ethical norms of their profession, current issues and challenges for the profession at large, and consideration of future directions for personal and professional development.

Enhancing professional vitality. New professionals are not the only ones who need new and different approaches, strategies, and knowledge. After a period of considerable expansion (Keim 1991), evidence is growing that the number of positions in student affairs is declining (Janasiewicz and Wright 1993). With growth in the number of professional positions followed by contraction, more professionals will reach the midpoint in their profession (and beyond) remaining at the same institution and perhaps in the same position. As a result, the need for an effective professional development program will be essential to maintain professional vitality.

Every profession contains a challenge to remain professionally vital—to maintain awareness of emerging issues and energetically integrate them with professional practice. Doing so is often difficult for the student affairs professional because of day-to-day demands. In every student affairs organization and for each professional, efforts must be made to identify and define professional development activities that continually expand professional vitality and capacity. Organizations and professionals should look for opportunities within the institution (cross-functional internships, leadership development activities like administrative fellowships for women and minorities, and graduate studies inside and outside traditional student affairs programs), within professional organizations (issue-oriented task forces, committees, and positions of leadership), and within the community (professional or business groups, opportunities for community service or leadership). Efforts to maintain vitality and avoid professional burnout are essential investments for each student affairs organization.

Continuing professional development for all staff. A number of issues are beginning to fill institutions' agendas for continuing professional development:

1. *Learning skills for collaborative problem solving.* The student affairs professional must have opportunities to become involved in the institution's efforts to develop comprehensive responses to complex problems and issues. A functional team (Jones 1988) or collaborative problem-solving approach enables student affairs professionals to serve both students and institutions while providing visibility as institutional experts on students and student-related institutional issues. To do so, student affairs professionals need traditional skills in interpersonal relations, group facilitation, and human development, along with more organizationally focused skills, such as planning and budgeting, and research and evaluation. Efforts to build these skills are essential in all student affairs organizations and in the profession generally.
2. *Applying technology.* Technological advances like computerization, voice mail, management information systems, telecommunications, electronic mail, and teleconferencing have the potential to enhance the productivity and effectiveness of student affairs staff substantially. Given rapid transformations in this area, regular updated training in the application of the latest technical innovations to traditional student affairs functions (such as student development) will prove invaluable to student affairs organizations (Watkins 1992).
3. *Reaching the community beyond the campus.* Tapping the potential of higher education to address social and community problems through special programs is emerging as a new role for student affairs professionals. In 1990, the federal government established the Commission on National and Community Service to award grants to colleges and universities for the development of links between college student services and social problems (Abdelnour 1992). To do so, student affairs professionals will need to learn to conceptualize student affairs in innovative ways to reach out to new populations not only on campus, but also within the community.
4. *Responding to the HIV/AIDS epidemic.* Although some colleges have sought to eliminate the involvement of HIV-positive students, legal and ethical considerations now require colleges to assume a more active role in involving these students (Cage 1992). Student affairs professionals must search for ways to educate and encourage all stu-

dents to assume an active responsibility for their own well-being. Current information, training in intervention and policy development, and additional resources, however, will be needed to facilitate efforts.

5. *Addressing violence on campus.* The acceleration in the amount of violence on campuses during the past few years has prompted such federal legislation as the Student Right to Know and Campus Security Act and the Sexual Assault Victims Bill of Rights. Colleges are now required to maintain and publish crime statistics and to actively respond to the needs of victims of campus violence. Student affairs professionals are challenged to identify and understand the dynamics of violence and find ways to decrease this alarming trend. To do so, staff will need training in conflict resolution, mediation, related legal and disciplinary issues, and strategies to identify and intervene before the violence intensifies.

6. *Fostering a multicultural campus.* With the changing student population, professionals must develop a greater awareness of the wide variations in the development, heritage, customs, and needs of the many underrepresented groups on campus. If student affairs professionals are to actively promote the development of all students, they will have to become familiar with theorists whose work has begun to explore the differences in the nature and process of the development of students who are not 17- to 22-year-old white males (Moore 1990; Wing, Arredondo, and McDavis 1992).

7. *Dealing with substance abuse.* Addressing this continuing problem has a renewed urgency, based on estimates that as many as 20 to 30 percent of the cases seen at college mental health facilities could involve problematic use of alcohol or other drugs (Grayson 1989) and the clear links between substance abuse and violence. The Drug-Free Schools and Communities Act amendments now require that every college or university receiving federal funds establish a drug and alcohol prevention program (Palmer, Gehring, and Guthrie 1992). Student affairs professionals need to be skilled in recognizing the signs of substance abuse, confronting students to facilitate a successful referral, and addressing improper behaviors through discipline.

Summary

The evolving role for student affairs professionals as integrators demands new and enhanced skills, placing special demands on graduate education for the profession. Existing preparation programs need to be revised in light of an expanding role for student affairs professionals. Similarly, continuing professional education must address the ongoing needs for new and enhanced skills and competencies. New efforts in graduate preparation and continuing professional education are critical, not only to the fulfillment of challenging new roles, but also to the future viability of the profession.

CONCLUSIONS AND RECOMMENDATIONS

The world of higher education is rarely static; changes in society, the higher education enterprise, and students themselves demand effective institutional responses. As a result, the role of student affairs is evolving to one that is more central and critical to the achievement of other institutional goals, to one that seeks a greater integration of efforts by all within the institution, to one that is concerned about organizational development as a necessary complement to student development. As integrators, student affairs professionals must address both the institution's and students' needs and goals by developing and integrating a wide range of skills, exerting leadership in new contexts, and thinking of themselves in new ways.

Student affairs leaders cannot afford to be isolationists.

Recognizing a new role for student affairs calls for responses by the profession: its professional organization, graduate preparation programs, and institutions seeking to maximize institutional effectiveness and vitality. The individual professional should not be alone in arguing his or her case for an expanded voice; recognition of this new role must be enabled by preparation programs, institutions, and professional associations.

From this new role and from recent efforts, a number of recommendations emerge. First, student affairs professionals must be prepared:

- **To assess the institutional environment.** Student affairs professionals must scan the environment to identify and interpret trends and events with implications for their institution and for student affairs. These trends include demographic changes, societal changes, economic trends, and the institution's political context. Student affairs leaders in this decade cannot afford to be isolationists.
- **To foster collaborative problem solving.** Student affairs leaders must be able to understand the important issues within their institutions and be prepared to interpret their implications for student affairs, to suggest ways in which student affairs can take leadership, and to alert others to important issues that must be addressed. Perhaps most important, student affairs professionals must be able to lead effectively in the development of comprehensive institutional responses to complex problems and issues.
- **To develop professional credibility with faculty.** To gain credibility with faculty, student affairs profession-

als must contribute in significant ways to the academic experience, document such effects, and articulate their importance to faculty colleagues. Research and evaluation should build the capacity of student affairs professionals to present hard data on the importance of their efforts. Student affairs leaders should capitalize on the importance of students' involvement as an opportunity to build relationships with faculty.

• **To disseminate strategic information on students and their expectations, needs, interests, and abilities.** Despite being the experts on students on campus, student affairs professionals often make little attempt to share their expertise with others. They must, however, more actively articulate that expertise to others in the institution. To be viewed as experts, they must ground rich anecdotal understandings in systematic studies, assessments, and evaluations.

• **To translate goals for student affairs to others in the institution in meaningful terms.** While institutions tend to share a culture, different units within even the smallest of institutions share different personal and professional values. It is essential to understand those underlying values and to be able to translate goals for student affairs in terms that are meaningful to others who possess a different set of values. To financial officers, for example, efforts to improve retention might be explained in terms of financial benefits; similarly, those efforts should be explained to faculty in terms of academic achievement.

• **To contribute to the quality of the academic experience.** Despite concerns about budgets, institutions are still concerned with the quality of the academic experience. Student affairs professionals must create cost-effective ways to provide meaningful academic experiences, such as community service and service learning.

• **To contribute to the effective and efficient management of institutions.** Student affairs leaders must understand and manage their organizations effectively to contribute to the overall productivity of the institution, including effective management of human and financial resources, planning, evaluation and assessment, quality management, and cost containment. As leaders in efforts to forge comprehensive responses to complex institutional problems and issues, student affairs professionals must develop greater understanding of institutional costs, program effectiveness, and outcomes.

• **To develop skills for a broader role.** Student affairs professionals, to meet challenging new roles as environmental scanners, milieu managers, market analysts, development officers, legal advisers, and quality assurance specialists, must develop a broader array of skills, including planning and budgeting, research and evaluation, and quality management.

To accomplish these goals, student affairs professionals must be supported by their institutions. Therefore, institutions should seek:

• **To recognize, enhance, and support the efforts of student affairs.** Effective student affairs programs are essential to an institution's survival and vitality, to the goals of a quality education, and to the institution's service to society. This evidence should be brought to the attention of all within the institution as it seeks to address present and future challenges creatively.

• **To consider student affairs full partners in the institution.** Along with a recognition of the real and potential accomplishments of student affairs must come a recognition that a stronger role for student affairs in the institution will contribute to the institution's vitality and effectiveness in new ways. Student affairs professionals *can* take leadership in areas beyond their typical roles.

• **To challenge student affairs professionals to make greater contributions.** Institutional leaders should expect student affairs staff to become more than disciplinarians, custodians, and educators; they should expect them to integrate students' and the institution's needs and to contribute meaningfully to institutional vitality. Institutional leaders should challenge them to develop the outlook, skills, and vision to look beyond their present roles.

To fulfill an expanded role, student affairs professionals need to develop a wider array of skills, and building skills begins in preparation programs; therefore, graduate programs must:

- **Develop present and future skills for the profession.** To be an effective student affairs professional calls for effective integration of skills necessary to promote both organizational development and student development. Common learning in preparation programs should address organizational and student development theory, counseling and human relations skills, planning and management skills, and research and evaluation.

And the professional associations representing student affairs professionals, such as the National Association of Student Personnel Administrators (NASPA), the American College Personnel Association (ACPA), the Association of College Unions–International (ACU-I), and the National Association of College Admissions Counselors (NACAC), for example, should continue to provide leadership for the profession as its evolves to meet new roles. Specifically, the national associations and their regional and state affiliates must:

- **Continue to provide direction for the profession.** National associations should define and emphasize the changing role of student affairs and recognize those efforts where student affairs staff contribute in significant ways to the development of the profession and the vitality of institutions.
- **Promote continuing professional development at all levels.** While the continuing professional development needs of novices and experienced professionals differ, national associations should build on efforts established to help young professionals define their professional goals, broaden the range of skills needed by middle managers, and provide opportunities for leadership for experienced professionals. Activities should be promoted at individual, institutional, state, regional, and national levels. Associations representing student affairs professionals must take the leadership in designing efforts to meet the continuing professional development needs of a profession in transition.

If forces are joined, a new future for the profession can be realized, one with substantial benefits for students, institutions, the student affairs profession, and higher education.

To do so will require significant effort—particularly on the part of student affairs professionals—but while the effort could be great, so too will the rewards.

REFERENCES

The Educational Resources Information Center (ERIC) Clearinghouse on Higher Education abstracts and indexes the current literature on higher education for inclusion in ERIC's data base and announcement in ERIC's monthly bibliographic journal, *Resources in Education* (RIE). Most of these publications are available through the ERIC Document Reproduction Service (EDRS). For publications cited in this bibliography that are available from EDRS, ordering number and price code are included. Readers who wish to order a publication should write to the ERIC Document Reproduction Service, 7420 Fullerton Rd., Suite 110, Springfield, VA 22153-2852. (Phone orders with VISA or MasterCard are taken at 800-443-ERIC or 703-440-1400.) When ordering, please specify the document (ED) number. Documents are available as noted in microfiche (MF) and paper copy (PC). If you have the price code ready when you call EDRS, an exact price can be quoted. The last page of the latest issue of *Resources in Education* also has the current cost, listed by code.

Abdelnour, A. 1992. "Programs for Community Service Get U.S. Aid." *Chronicle of Higher Education* 39: A28.

Adelman, C. 1991. *Women at Thirtysomething: Paradoxes of Attainment.* Washington, D.C.: U.S. Dept. of Education, Office of Educational Research and Improvement. ED 338 532. 79 pp. MF–01; PC–04.

Allen, K.E., and E.L. Garb. 1993. "Reinventing Student Affairs: Something Old and Something New." *NASPA Journal* 30: 93–100.

American Council on Education. 1937. *The Student Personnel Point of View: Report of a Conference.* Washington, D.C.: Author.

———. 1949. *The Student Personnel Point of View.* Rev. ed. Washington, D.C.: Author.

Andreas, R., and L. Krager. 1989. "Dissemination of a Student Development Model within a Student Life Unit." Paper presented at the Arizona ACPA/NASPA Joint Conference, Tucson.

Appleton, J., C. Briggs, and J. Rhatigan. 1978. *Pieces of Eight.* Portland, Ore.: National Association of Student Personnel Administrators. ED 292 432. 195 pp. MF–01; PC–08.

Astin, A.W. 1977. *Four Critical Years.* San Francisco: Jossey-Bass.

———. 1984. "Student Involvement: A Developmental Theory for Higher Education." *Journal of College Student Personnel* 25: 297–308.

———. 1985. *Achieving Educational Excellence: A Critical Assessment of Priorities and Practices in Higher Education.* San Francisco: Jossey-Bass.

———. 1990. *Assessment for Excellence: The Philosophy and Practice of Assessment and Evaluation in Higher Education.* New York: Macmillan.

———. 1992. *What Matters in College: Four Critical Years Revisited.*

San Francisco: Jossey-Bass.

Astin, A.W., E.L. Dey, W.S. Korn, and E. Riggs. 1992. *The American Freshman: National Norms for Fall 1992.* Los Angeles: UCLA, Higher Education Research Institute. ED 352 891. 271 pp. MF–01; PC–11.

Astone, B., and E. Nuñez-Wormack. 1990. *Pursuing Diversity: Recruiting College Minority Students.* ASHE-ERIC Higher Education Report No. 7. Washington, D.C.: George Washington Univ., School of Education and Human Development. ED 333 867. 103 pp. MF–01; PC–05.

Bagasao, P.Y. 1989. "Student Voices. Breaking the Silence: The Asian and Pacific American Experience." *Change* 21: 20–28.

Baier, John L. 1993. "Technological Change in Student Affairs Administration." In *The Handbook of Student Affairs Administration,* edited by Margaret J. Barr and Associates. San Francisco: Jossey-Bass.

Baldridge, J. Victor, Frank R. Kemerer, and Kenneth C. Green. 1982. *The Enrollment Crisis: Factors, Actors, and Impacts.* AAHE-ERIC Higher Education Report No. 3. Washington, D.C.: American Association for Higher Education. ED 222 158. 79 pp. MF–01; PC–04.

Banning, J.H. 1989. "The Campus Ecology Manager Role." In *Student Services: A Handbook for the Profession,* edited by Ursula Delworth, Gary Hanson, and Associates. 2d ed. San Francisco: Jossey-Bass.

Barlett, Donald L., and James B. Steele. 1992. *America: What Went Wrong?* Kansas City: Andrews & McMeel.

Barr, M.J. 1988. "Managing the Enterprise." In *Managing Student Affairs Effectively,* edited by Margaret J. Barr, M. Lee Upcraft, and Associates. New Directions for Student Services No. 41. San Francisco: Jossey-Bass.

———. 1993. "Becoming a Successful Student Affairs Administrator." In *The Handbook of Student Affairs Administration,* edited by Margaret J. Barr and Associates. San Francisco: Jossey-Bass.

Barr, M.J., M.L. Upcraft, and Associates. 1990. *New Futures for Student Affairs: Building a Vision for Professional Leadership and Practice.* San Francisco: Jossey-Bass.

Baxter-Magolda, M.B. 1990. "Gender Difference in Epistemological Development." *Journal of College Student Development* 31: 555–63.

———. 1992. "Co-curricular Influences on College Students' Intellectual Development." *Journal of College Student Development* 33(2): 203–13.

Beatty, D.L., and L.C. Stamatakos. 1990. "Faculty and Administrator Perceptions of Knowledge, Skills, and Competencies as Standards for Doctoral Preparation Programs in Student Affairs Administration." *Journal of College Student Development* 31: 221–29.

Bloland, P. 1986. "Student Development: The New Orthodoxy." *ACPA Developments* 13: 1–22.

Bodinger-Deuriarte, Cristina, and Anthony R. Sancho. 1991. *Hate Crimes: A Sourcebook for Schools Confronting Bigotry, Harassment, Vandalism, and Violence.* Los Alamitos, Calif.: Southwestern Regional Laboratory for Education Research and Evaluation. ED 334 523. 110 pp. MF–01; PC–05.

Bok, D. 1986. *Higher Education.* Cambridge, Mass.: Harvard Univ. Press.

———. 1992. "Reclaiming the Public Trust." *Change* 24: 12–19.

Borland, David T. 1980. "Organizational Development: A Professional Imperative." In *Student Development in Higher Education,* edited by Don G. Creamer. Cincinnati: American College Personnel Association.

Boyer, E.L. 1987. *College: The Undergraduate Experience in America.* For the Carnegie Foundation for the Advancement of Teaching. New York: Harper & Row.

Brazziel, William F. 1989. "Older Students." In *Shaping Higher Education's Future: Demographic Realities and Opportunities, 1900–2000,* edited by Arthur Levine and Associates. San Francisco: Jossey-Bass.

Bricketto, M.J. 1989. "Using Change Strategies to Involve Faculty in Student Affairs." *NASPA Journal* 27: 95–101.

Brodzinski, Frederick R. 1978. "The Future of Student Services: Parameters, Resources, and Consumer Interests." Paper presented at the First National Conference on Student Services, October, Madison, Wisconsin. ED 175 327. 30 pp. MF–01; PC–02.

Brown, Charles. 1991. "Increasing Minority Access to College: Seven Efforts for Success." *NASPA Journal* 28: 224–30.

Brown, R.D. 1972. *Student Development in Tomorrow's Higher Education: A Return to the Academy.* Student Personnel Series No. 16. Washington, D.C.: American College Personnel Association.

———. 1985. "Graduate Education for the Student Development Educator: A Content and Process Model." *NASPA Journal* 22: 38–43.

Brown, R.D., and M.J. Barr. 1990. "Student Development: Yesterday, Today, and Tomorrow." In *Evolving Theoretical Perspectives on Students,* edited by Leila Moore. New Directions for Student Services No. 51. San Francisco: Jossey-Bass.

Brown, V.L., and D.A. DeCoster. 1989. "The Disturbed and Disturbing Student." In *Dealing with the Behavioral and Psychological Problems of Students,* edited by Ursula Delworth. New Directions for Student Services No. 45. San Francisco: Jossey-Bass.

Brubacher, J.S., and W. Rudy. 1976. *Higher Education in Transition.* New York: Harper & Row.

Bucci, Frank A. 1993. " 'Student Personnel: All Hail and Farewell!'

Revisited." *NASPA Journal* 30: 169–75.

Bustamante, A.M. 1992. "College Student Sexual Knowledge and Behavior in the AIDS Era." *Journal of College Student Development* 33: 376–78.

Cage, M.C. 1992. "To Shield Academic Programs from Cuts, Many Colleges Pare Student Services." *Chronicle of Higher Education* 39: A25–A26.

Canon, H.J. 1984. "Developmental Tasks for the Profession: The Next 25 Years." *Journal of College Student Personnel* 25: 105–11.

Caple, R.B., and F.B. Newton. 1991. "Leadership in Student Affairs." In *Administration and Leadership in Student Affairs: Actualizing Student Development in Higher Education,* edited by T.K. Miller, R.B. Winston, and Associates. Muncie, Ind.: Accelerated Development, Inc.

Carnegie Council on Policy Studies in Higher Education. 1980. *Three Thousand Futures.* San Francisco: Jossey-Bass.

Carnegie Foundation for the Advancement of Teaching. 1989. *The Condition of the Professoriate: Attitudes and Trends, 1989.* Technical report. Princeton, N.J.: Author.

Carter, D., and D.R. Merkowitz. 1993. *11th Annual Status Report on Minorities in Higher Education.* Washington, D.C.: American Council on Education.

Cartwright, C.A. 1992. "Reclaiming the Public Trust: A Look to the Future." *AAHE Bulletin* 44: 14–16.

Chabotar, K.J., and J.P. Honan. 1990. "Coping with Retrenchment: Strategies and Tactics." *Change* 22: 28–34.

Cheatham, H.E., and Associates. 1991. *Cultural Pluralism on Campus.* Alexandria, Va.: American College Personnel Association. ED 338 929. 216 pp. MF–01; PC not available EDRS.

Chronicle of Higher Education. 13 January 1993a. "Colleges Eager to Take Part in Clinton's National-Service Program" 39: A24.

———. 3 March 1993b. "1991 Enrollments at 3,100 Institutions of Higher Education" 39 (26): A31–A39.

Cibik, Margaret A., and Stephen L. Chambers. 1991. "Similarities and Differences among Native Americans, Hispanics, Blacks, and Anglos." *NASPA Journal* 28: 129–39.

Clement, L.M., and S.T. Rickard. 1992. *Effective Leadership in Student Services: Voices from the Field.* San Francisco: Jossey-Bass.

Cloud, R.C. 1992. "The President and the Law." *Educational Record* 73: 8–15.

Committee on Education and Labor. 1990. *Hearings on H.R. 3344, The Crime Awareness and Campus Security Act of 1989.* U.S. Congress, House of Representatives. Washington, D.C.: Author.

Cope, Robert G. 1981. *Strategic Planning, Management, and Decision Making.* AAHE-ERIC Higher Education Report No. 9. Washington, D.C.: American Association for Higher Education. ED 217 825.

75 pp. MF–01; PC–03.

Cornesky, R., S. McCool, L. Brynes, and R. Weber. 1991. *Implementing TQM in Higher Education.* Madison, Wis.: Magna Publications. ED 343 535. 154 pp. MF–01; PC not available EDRS.

Council for Aid to Education. 1991. *Voluntary Support of Education.* Vol. 1. Estimates and Survey. New York: Author.

Coupland, Douglas. 1991. *Generation X.* New York: St. Martin's Press.

Cowley, W.H. 1949. *Student Development in Higher Education: Theories, Practices, and Future Directions.* Washington, D.C.: American College Personnel Association.

Cox, D.W., and W.A. Ivy. 1984. "Staff Development Needs of Student Affairs Professionals." *NASPA Journal* 22: 26–33.

Creamer, D.G., and Marcia Shelton. 1988. "Staff Development: A Literature Review of Graduate Preparation and In-service Education of Students." *Journal of College Student Development* 32: 407–13.

Creamer, E.G., and D.G. Creamer. 1991. "Construct Reliability of the Probability of Adoption of Change (PAC) Model." *Journal of College Student Development* 32: 1–38.

Crookston, B.B. 1975. "Milieu Management." *NASPA Journal* 13: 45–55.

———. 1976. "Student Personnel: All Hail and Farewell!" *Personnel and Guidance Journal* 55: 26–29.

DeBevoise, W. 1986. "Collaboration: Some Principles of Bridgework." *Educational Leadership* 43: 9–12.

Deegan, William L. 1981. *Managing Student Affairs Programs: Methods, Models, and Muddles.* Palm Springs, Calif.: ETC Publications.

Delve, Cecilia I., Suzanne D. Mintz, and M. Stewart Greig, eds. 1990. *Community Service as Values Education.* New Directions for Student Services No. 50. San Francisco: Jossey-Bass.

Delworth, Ursula R., ed. 1989. *Dealing with the Behavioral and Psychological Problems of Students.* New Directions for Student Services No. 45. San Francisco: Jossey-Bass.

Delworth, U.R., G.R. Hanson, and Associates, eds. 1989. *Student Services: A Handbook for the Profession.* 2d ed. San Francisco: Jossey-Bass.

Demetrulias, Diana A.M., Joan L. Sattler, and Leslie P. Graham. Summer 1992. "How Do You Know When You Are Hungry? Disabled Students in University Settings." *Journal of NAWDAC* 45: 8–13.

DeWitt, R.C. 1991. "Managing a Student Affairs Team: It's a New Ball Game." *NASPA Journal* 28: 185–88.

Dey, Eric L., Alexander W. Astin, and William S. Korn. 1991. *The American Freshman: Twenty-five Year Trends, 1966–1990.* Los Angeles: UCLA, Higher Education Research Institute. ED 340 325. 219 pp.

MF–01; PC not available EDRS.

Dickson, G.L. 1991. "Developmental Theory and Organizational Structure: An Integration." *NASPA Journal* 28: 202–15.

Ebbers, L.H., and S.L. Henry. 1990. "Cultural Competence: A New Challenge to Student Affairs Professionals." *NASPA Journal* 27(4): 319–23.

Ebbers, L.H., and B.J. Kruempel. 1992. "Student Affairs Preparation Programs: Should They Be Accredited?" *NASPA Journal* 30: 59–65.

Erwin, T. Daryl, and Stephen Miller. Spring 1985. "Technology and the Three Rs." *NASPA Journal* 22: 47–51.

Evangelauf, J. 21 October 1992. "Tuition at Public Colleges and Universities Is Up 10% This Year, College Board Study Finds." *Chronicle of Higher Education* 39: A36.

————. 20 January 1993. "Number of Minority Students in College Rose by 9% from 1990 to 1991, U.S. Reports." *Chronicle of Higher Education* 39: A30–A31.

Evans, N.J. 1988. "Attrition of Student Affairs Professionals: A Review of the Literature." *Journal of College Student Development* 29: 19–24.

Fenske, R.H. 1989. "Evolution of the Student Services Profession." In *Student Services: A Handbook for the Profession,* edited by Ursula R. Delworth, Gary R. Hanson, and Associates. 2d ed. San Francisco: Jossey-Bass.

Fenske, R.H., and Edward A. Johnson. 1990. "Changing Regulatory and Legal Environments." In *New Futures for Student Affairs,* edited by Margaret Barr, M. Lee Upcraft, and Associates. San Francisco: Jossey-Bass.

Finn, Cester E., Jr. 1988. "Judgment Time for Higher Education in the Court of Public Opinion." *Change* 20: 35–39.

Fiske, Edward B. 1988. "The Undergraduate Hispanic Experience." *Change* 20: 29–33.

Foxley, Cecilia H., ed. 1980. *Applying Management Techniques.* New Directions for Student Services No. 9. San Francisco: Jossey-Bass.

Frances, Carole, and James Harrison. 1993. "The Impact of the Federal Budget Deficit on Student Aid Funding." *Higher Education Extension Service Review* 4: 1–11.

Frank, Keith, and Pat Wade. 1993. "Disabled Student Services in Postsecondary Education: Who's Responsible for What?" *Journal of College Student Development* 34(1): 26–30.

Frost, Susan W. 1991. *Academic Advising for Student Success: A System of Shared Responsibility.* ASHE-ERIC Higher Education Report No. 3. Washington, D.C.: George Washington Univ., School of Education and Human Development. ED 339 272. 118 pp. MF–01; PC–05.

Gallagher, S.P. 1989. "The Juggling Act of the College Counseling

Center: A Point of View." *Counseling Psychologist* 17: 477–89.

Garland, P.H. 1991. "State Initiatives to Enhance Teaching and Learn-ing." Paper presented at the National Conference on Enhancing the Quality of Teaching in Colleges and Universities, February 1–3, Charleston, South Carolina. ED 350 910. 20 pp. MF–01; PC–01.

Gayle, H.D., R.P. Keeling, M. Garcia-Tunon, B.W. Kilbourne, J.P. Nar-kunas, F.R. Ingram, M.F. Rogers, and J.W. Curran. 29 November 1990. "Prevalence of the Human Immunodeficiency Virus among University Students." *New England Journal of Medicine* 3-93: 1538–41.

Gerald, Debra E., and William J. Hussar. 1992. *Projections of Edu-cation Statistics to 2003.* Washington, D.C.: U.S. Dept. of Education, National Center for Education Statistics. ED 354 256. 182 pp. MF–01; PC–08.

Giddan, N.S., and S.J. Weiss. 1990. "Costs and Effectiveness of Coun-seling Center Dropout Prevention." *Journal of College Student Development* 31: 100–107.

Gilbert, S.P. 1992. "Ethical Issues in the Treatment of Severe Psycho-pathology in University and College Counseling Centers." *Journal of Counseling and Development* 70: 695–700.

Gordon, S.E., C.B. Strode, and B.A. Mann. 1993. "The Mid-Manager in Student Affairs: What Are CSAOs Looking For?" *NASPA Journal* 30: 290–97.

Gordon, S.E., and D. Weist. 1988. "Critical Steps in Developing Pro-gram Evaluation for Student Services." *NASPA Journal* 26: 110–17.

Grayson, Paul. 1989. "The College Psychotherapy Client: An Over-view." In *College Psychotherapy,* edited by Paul Grayson and K. Cauley. New York: Guilford Press.

Green, Kenneth C. April 1983. "Retention: An Old Solution Finds a New Problem." *AAHE Bulletin* 35: 3–6.

———. 1989. "The Children of the Upheaval: A Look at Today's Col-lege Freshmen." *Journal of the Freshman Year Experience* 1: 20–42.

Greenberg, Arthur R. 1991. *High School–College Partnerships: Con-ceptual Models, Programs, and Issues.* ASHE-ERIC Higher Education Report No. 5. Washington, D.C.: George Washington Univ., School of Education and Human Development. ED 343 546. 125 pp. MF–01; PC–05.

Greenfeig, Beverly R., and Barbara J. Goldberg. 1984. "Orienting Returning Adult Students." In *Orienting Students to College,* edited by M. Lee Upcraft. New Directions for Student Services No. 25. San Francisco: Jossey-Bass.

Gunther, Gerald. 1990. "Freedom for the Thoughts We Hate." *Aca-deme* 76: 10–12.

Gurowitz, William D., William M.K. Trochim, and Howard C. Kramer.

1989. "A Process for Planning." *NASPA Journal* 25: 226–35.

Hackman, Judith Dozier. 1992. "What Is Going on in Higher Education? Is It Time for a Change?" *Review of Higher Education* 16: 10–17.

Hameister, Brenda. 1984. "Orienting Disabled Students." In *Orienting Students to College*, edited by M. Lee Upcraft. New Directions for Student Services No. 25. San Francisco: Jossey-Bass.

Hamrick, F.A., and L.W. Carlisle. 1990. "Gender Diversity in Student Affairs: Administrative Perceptions and Recommendations." *NASPA Journal* 27: 306–12.

Hansen, Janet S. 1987. *Student Loans: Are They Overburdening a Generation?* New York: College Board Publications.

Hanson, Gary R. 1990. "Improving Practice through Research, Evaluation, and Outcomes Assessment." In *New Futures for Student Affairs*, edited by Margaret Barr, M. Lee Upcraft, and Associates. San Francisco: Jossey-Bass.

Harrison, Patrick J., Jeanette Downes, and Michael D. Williams. 1991. "Date and Acquaintance Rape: Perceptions, Attitudes, and Change Strategies." *Journal of College Student Development* 32: 131–39.

Harvey, James. 1992. "Footing the Bill: Financial Prospects for Higher Education." *Educational Record* 73: 11–17.

Henderson, Cathy. 1992. *College Freshmen with Disabilities: A Statistical Profile.* Washington, D.C.: American Council on Education. ED 354 792. 43 pp. MF–01; PC–02.

Herr, E.L., and S.H. Cramer. 1979. *Career Guidance through the Life Span.* Boston: Little, Brown & Co.

Hexter, Holly, and Elaine El-Khawas. 1988. *Joining Forces: The Military's Impact on College Enrollments.* Washington, D.C.: American Council on Education.

Hines, Edward. 1992. *Appropriations: State Tax Funds for Operating Expenses of Higher Education, 1990–91.* Terre Haute: Indiana State Univ. ED 343 532. 44 pp. MF–01; PC–02.

Hintz, J.A., and L.C. Stamatakos. 1978. "Goal Congruence and Perceived Need for Greater Cooperation between Undergraduate Faculty and Student Affairs Staff." *Journal of College Student Personnel* 19: 146–52.

Hodgkinson, Harold L. 1991. "Higher Education, 1990–2010: A Demographic View." Occasional paper from the Center for Demographic Policy. Washington, D.C.: Institute for Education Leadership.

Hossler, D. 1985. "Enrollment Management: A Paradigm for Student Affairs Professionals." *NASPA Journal* 23: 2–8.

———, ed. 1991. *Evaluating Student Recruitment and Retention Programs.* New Directions for Institutional Research No. 70. San Francisco: Jossey-Bass.

Howe, Neil, and Bill Strauss. 1993. *13th Gen: Abort, Retry, Ignore,*

Fail? New York: Vintage Books.

Huebner, L.A. 1989. "Interaction of Student and Campus." In *Student Services: A Handbook for the Profession,* edited by Ursula R. Delworth, Gary R. Hanson, and Associates. 2d ed. San Francisco: Jossey-Bass.

Huebner, L.A., and J.M. Lawson. 1990. "Understanding and Assessing College Environments." In *College Student Development Theory and Practice for the 1990s,* edited by Don Creamer and Associates. Media Publication No. 49. Alexandria, Va.: American College Personnel Association.

Hughes, Rees. Winter 1983. "The Nontraditional Student in Higher Education: A Synthesis of the Literature." *NASPA Journal* 20: 51–64.

Hunter, D.E. 1992. "How Student Affairs Professionals Choose Their Careers." *NASPA Journal* 29: 181–88.

Hunter, D.E., and D. Comey. 1991. "Common Learning in Student Affairs." *NASPA Journal* 29: 10–16.

Hutchings, P., and T. Marchese. September/October 1990. "Watching Assessment: Questions, Stories, and Prospects." *Change* 22: 12–38.

Hyman, Randy, Alton Jamison, Mark Von Destinon, and Dudley B. Woodard. 1988. "Student Outcomes Assessment Survey, 1987–89." Paper presented at an annual meeting of the Association for the Study of Higher Education, November 4–6, St. Louis, Missouri. ED 294 487. 31 pp. MF–01; PC–02.

Immerwahr, John, and Steve Farkas. 1993. "The Closing Gateway: Californians Consider Their Higher Education System." San Jose: California Higher Education Policy Center.

Janasiewicz, B.A., and D.L. Wright. 1993. "Job Market Trends in Student Affairs: Ten Years Later." *NASPA Journal* 30(2): 145–52.

Jaschik, Scott. 1992. "1% Decline in State Support for College Thought to Be First 2-Year Drop Ever." *Chronicle of Higher Education* 39: A21.

Johnson, D.H., and B.H. Steele. 1984. "A National Survey of Research Activity and Attitudes in Student Affairs Divisions." *Journal of College Student Personnel* 25: 200–206.

Johnson, Sandra L., and Joel W. Meyerson. 1992. "Top Concerns for 1993." *AGB Reports* 34: 6.

Jones, Andrew C., Melvin C. Terrell, and Margaret Duggar. 1991. "The Role of Student Affairs in Fostering Diversity in Higher Education." *NASPA Journal* 28: 121–27.

Jones, D.J., and B.C. Watson. 1991. *High-Risk Students in Higher Education: Future Trends.* ASHE-ERIC Higher Education Report No. 3. Washington, D.C.: George Washington Univ., School of Education and Human Development. ED 321 726. 138 pp. MF–01; PC–06.

Jones, P.E. 1988. "Student Services Perspectives from a Different Point of View: Theory and Application of Functional Coordination." *NASPA Journal* 25: 213–17.

Kalantzis, M., and W. Cope. 1992. "Multiculturalism May Prove to Be the Key Issue of Our Epoch." *Chronicle of Higher Education* 38: B3.

Kaplan, W.A. 1992. *The Law of Higher Education.* San Francisco: Jossey-Bass.

Kasworm, C.E. March 1980. "Student Services for the Older Undergraduate Student." *Journal of College Student Personnel* 21: 163–69.

Katz, J. 1989. "The Challenge of Diversity." In *Valuing Diversity,* edited C. Woolbright. Bloomington, Ind.: Association of College Unions–International.

Keim, M.C. 1991. "Student Personnel Preparation Programs: A Longitudinal Study." *NASPA Journal* 28(3): 231–42.

Keller, George C. 1983. *Academic Strategy: The Management Revolution in American Higher Education.* Baltimore: Johns Hopkins Univ. Press.

Kinnick, Bernard C., and R.L. Bolheimer. Fall 1984. "College Presidents' Perceptions of Student Affairs Issues and Development Needs of Chief Student Affairs Officers." *NASPA Journal* 22: 2–9.

Knefelkamp, L., C. Widick, and C. Parker. 1978. *Applying New Developmental Findings.* San Francisco: Jossey-Bass.

Komives, Susan R. 1992. "The Middles: Observations on Professional Competence and Autonomy." *Journal of College Student Development* 29: 83–90.

Kozloff, Jessica. 1987. "A Student-Centered Approach to Accountability and Assessment." *Journal of College Student Personnel* 28: 419–24.

Kuh, George D. Spring 1981a. "Beyond Student Development: Contemporary Priorities for Student Affairs." *NASPA Journal* 18: 29–36.

———. 1981b. *Indices of Quality in the Undergraduate Experience.* AAHE-ERIC Higher Education Report No. 4. Washington, D.C.: American Association for Higher Education. ED 213 340. 50 pp. MF–01; PC–02.

———. 1985. "What Is Extraordinary about Ordinary Student Affairs Organizations?" *NASPA Journal* 23: 31–43.

Kuh, G.D., and R. Andreas. 1991. "It's about Time: Using Qualitative Methods in Student Life Studies." *Journal of College Student Development* 32: 397–405.

Kuh, G.D., N. Evans, and A. Duke. 1983. "Career Paths and Responsibilities of Chief Student Affairs Officers." *NASPA Journal* 21: 39–47.

Kuk, L. 1990. "Perspectives on Gender Differences." In *Evolving Theoretical Perspectives on Students,* edited by Leila Moore. San Francisco: Jossey-Bass.

Kuyper, L.A. 1987. "Career Development of Women in Administration of Higher Education: Contributing Factors." *Journal of NAWDAC* 50: 3–7.

Laramee, William A. 1992. "Racism, Group Defamation, and Freedom of Speech on Campus." *NASPA Journal* 29: 55–62.

Lawrence, Charles R., III. 1990. "Acknowledging the Victim's Cry." *Academe* 76: 6.

Lazerson, Marvin, and Ursula Wagener. 1992. "Rethinking How Colleges Operate." *Chronicle of Higher Education* 39: A44.

Lenning, Oscar T. 1989. "Assessment and Evaluation." In *Student Services: A Handbook for the Profession,* edited by Ursula R. Delworth, Gary R. Hanson, and Associates. 2d ed. San Francisco: Jossey-Bass.

Leslie, Larry L., and H.F. Miller, Jr. 1974. *Higher Education and the Steady State.* AAHE-ERIC Higher Education Report No. 4. Washington, D.C.: American Association for Higher Education. ED 091 965. 65 pp. MF–01; PC–03.

Levin, M.E., and J.R. Levin. 1991. "A Critical Examination of Academic Retention Programs for At-risk Minority College Students." *Journal of College Student Development* 32: 323–34.

Levine, Arthur. 1980. *When Dreams and Heroes Died.* San Francisco: Jossey-Bass.

———. 1993. "The Making of a Generation." *Change* 25(4): 8–15.

Levine, Arthur, and Deborah Hirsch. 1990. "Student Activism and Optimism Return to the Campuses." *Chronicle of Higher Education:* A48.

Levine, Arthur, and Associates. 1989. *Shaping Higher Education's Future: Demographic Realities and Opportunities, 1990–2000.* San Francisco: Jossey-Bass.

Ludeman, Roger B., and Richard Fisher. 1989. "Breathe Life into Student Life with CPR: Comprehensive Program Review." *NASPA Journal* 26: 4.

Mable, P., and T.K. Miller. 1991. "Standards of Professional Practice." In *Administration and Leadership in Student Affairs: Actualizing Student Development in Higher Education,* edited by T.K. Miller, R.B. Winston, and Associates. Muncie, Ind.: Accelerated Development, Inc.

McComas, James D. 1989. "Student Affairs Leadership Role in the Reform of Undergraduate Education." *NASPA Journal* 27: 7–10.

McConnell, T.R. 1970. "Student Personnel Services: Central or Peripheral?" *NASPA Journal* 8: 55–63.

McEwen, M.K., T.E. Williams, and C.M. Engstom. 1991. "Feminization in Student Affairs: A Qualitative Investigation." *Journal of College*

Student Development 32: 440–46.

McIntire, R.W., D.K. Pumroy, M.L. Burgee, S.R. Alexander, S.S. Gerson, and A.M. Saddoris. 1992. "Improving Retention through Intensive Practice in College Survival Skills." *Journal of College Student Development* 29: 299–306.

McPherson, Michael S., and Morton O. Schapiro. 1990. "Projections of College Costs and Affordability." Williamstown, Mass.: Williams College, The Williams Project on the Economics of Higher Education.

Malaney, G.D., and W.H. Weitzer. 1993. "Research on Students: A Framework of Methods Based on Cost and Expertise." *NASPA Journal* 30: 126–37.

Manning, K., and P. Coleman-Boatwright. 1991. "Student Affairs Initiatives toward a Multicultural University." *Journal of College Student Development* 32: 374.

Matthews, Jana B., and Rolf Norgaard. 1984. *Managing the Partnership between Higher Education and Industry.* Boulder, Colo.: NCHEMS.

Miller, T.K., and J.S. Prince. 1976. *The Future of Student Affairs.* San Francisco: Jossey-Bass.

Miller, T.K., R.B. Winston, and Associates. 1991. *Administration and Leadership in Student Affairs: Actualizing Student Development in Higher Education.* 2d ed. Muncie, Ind.: Accelerated Development, Inc.

Mingle, James R. 1992. "Low Tuition, Progressive Taxation." *AGB Reports* 34: 6.

Minter, John. 1991. "Fiscal Facts, Trends, and Forecasts." *Educational Record* 72: 2.

Mohrman, K. Fall 1987. "Unintended Consequences of Federal Student Aid Policies." *Brookings Review* 5(4): 24–30.

Moore, L.V. 1990. *Evolving Theoretical Perspectives on Students.* New Directions for Student Services No. 51. San Francisco: Jossey-Bass.

Morse, Suzanne W. 1989. *Renewing Civic Capacity: Preparing College Students for Service and Citizenship.* ASHE-ERIC Higher Education Report No. 8. Washington, D.C.: George Washington Univ., School of Education and Human Development. ED 320 524. 148 pp. MF–01; PC–06.

Mortimer, Kenneth P., and Michael L. Tierney. 1979. *The Three "R's" of the Eighties: Reduction, Retrenchment, and Reallocation.* AAHE-ERIC Higher Education Report No. 4. Washington, D.C.: American Association for Higher Education. ED 172 642. 93 pp. MF–01; PC–04.

Mumper, Michael. 1993. "The Affordability of Public Higher Education: 1970–90." *Review of Higher Education* 16(2): 157–80.

National Association of Student Personnel Administrators. 1987. *A Perspective on Student Affairs.* Iowa City: ACT Services.

National Commission on Excellence in Education. 1983. *A Nation at Risk.* Washington, D.C.: National Institute of Education. ED 226 006. 72 pp. MF–01; PC–03.

Noel, L., R. Levitz, D. Saluri, and Associates, eds. 1985. *Increasing Student Retention.* San Francisco: Jossey-Bass.

O'Brien, Eileen M. 1992. *Part-time Enrollments: Trends and Issues.* 1992 Research Brief Series. Washington, D.C.: American Council on Education. ED 353 872. 92 pp. MF–01; PC–04.

Oetting, E.R. 1967. "A Developmental Definition of Counseling Psychology." *Journal of Counseling Psychology* 14: 382–85.

Orfield, Gary. 1989. "Hispanics." In *Shaping Higher Education's Future: Demographic Realities and Opportunities, 1900–2000,* edited by Arthur Levine and Associates. San Francisco: Jossey-Bass.

Palmer, C.J., D.D. Gehring, and V.L. Guthrie. 1992. "Students' Knowledge of Information Mandated by the 1989 Amendments to the Drug Free Schools and Communities Act." *NASPA Journal* 30(1): 30–38.

Pascarella, E. 1985. "College Environmental Influences on Learning and Cognitive Development: A Critical Review and Synthesis." In *Higher Education: Handbook of Theory and Research,* vol. 1, edited by John Smart. New York: Agathon.

Pascarella, E., and P.T. Terenzini. 1991. *How College Affects Students: Findings and Insights from Twenty Years of Research.* San Francisco: Jossey-Bass.

Pavela, G. 1985. *The Dismissal of Students with Mental Disorders.* Asheville, N.C.: College Administration Publications.

Peng, Samuel S. 1990. "Some Selected Statistics on Higher Education: What Do They Signify?" Paper presented at an annual meeting of the American Educational Research Association, April 8, Boston, Massachusetts.

Piper, T.D., and R.F. Rodgers. 1992. "Theory-Practice Congruence: Factors Influencing the Internalization of Theory." *Journal of College Student Development* 33: 117–23.

Porter, J. 1989. "Leadership and Ownership within Student Affairs." *NASPA Journal* 27: 11–17.

Presidential Task Force on Alcohol and Other Drug Use. 1992. *Drugs on Campus at the Bimillennium.* Harrisburg: Pennsylvania Association of Colleges and Universities.

Presley, C.A., and P.W. Meilman. 1992. *Alcohol and Drugs on American College Campuses.* Washington, D.C.: CORE Institute. ED 350 931. 24 pp. MF–01; PC–01.

Rhatigan, J.J. 1975. "Student Services vs. Student Development: Is There a Difference?" *Journal of NAWDAC* 8: 51–59.

Richardson, Richard C., Jr., and Elizabeth F. Skinner. 1990. "Adapting to Diversity: Organizational Influences on Student Achievement." *Journal of Higher Education* 61: 486–510.

Robinson, Sharon E., Alberta M. Gloria, Sari L. Roth, and Renee M.

Schuetter. 1993. "Patterns of Drug Use among Female and Male Undergraduates." *Journal of College Student Development* 34: 130–37.

Rodgers, R.F. 1983. "Current Issues in Student Affairs and Higher Education." Panel presentation at an annual conference of NASPA. Toronto, Ontario.

———. 1991. "Using Theory in Practice in Student Affairs." In *Administration and Leadership in Student Affairs: Actualizing Student Development in Higher Education,* edited by T.K. Miller, R.B. Winston, and Associates. Muncie, Ind.: Accelerated Development, Inc.

Rollin, Roger. 1989. "There's No Business Like Education." *Academe* 75: 14–17.

Rudolph, Frederick. 1962. *The American College and University.* New York: Vintage Books.

Russell, Alene Bycer. 1992. *Faculty Workload: State and System Perspectives.* Denver: State Higher Education Executive Officers. ED 356 728. 82 pp. MF–01; PC–04.

Ryan, Mark B. 1992. "Residential Colleges: A Legacy of Living and Learning Together." *Change* 24: 5.

Sagaria, M.A., and L.K. Johnsrud. 1991. "Recruiting, Advancing, and Retaining Minorities in Student Affairs: Moving from Rhetoric to Results." *NASPA Journal* 28: 105–20.

St. John, E.P., R.J. Kirshtein, and J. Noell. 1991. "The Effects of Student Financial Aid on Persistence." *Review of Higher Education* 14: 383–406.

Samuels, James E. 1989. "The Emergence of Proactive University Counsel in the 1990s." *Journal for Higher Education Management* 5: 45–52.

Sandeen, Arthur. 1991. *The Chief Student Affairs Officer.* San Francisco: Jossey-Bass.

Schlossberg, N.K., A.Q. Lynch, and A.W. Chickering. 1989. *Improving Higher Education Environments for Adults: Responsive Programs and Services from Entry to Departure.* San Francisco: Jossey-Bass.

Seldin, P., and Associates. 1990. *How Administrators Can Improve Teaching.* San Francisco: Jossey-Bass.

Seymour, Daniel T. 1991. "TQM on Campus: What the Pioneers Are Finding." *AAHE Bulletin* 44(3): 10–13. ED 340 270. 6 pp. MF–01; PC–01.

Shaffer, R.H. 1973. "An Emerging Role of Student Personnel: Contributing to Organizational Effectiveness." *Journal of College Student Personnel* 14: 386–91.

———. 1984. "Critical Dimensions of Student Affairs in the Decades Ahead." *Journal of College Student Personnel* 25: 112–14.

———. 1987. "Student Affairs: Retrospect and Prospect." Paper presented at a joint conference of the American College Personnel Association and the National Association of Student Personnel

Administrators, March, Chicago, Illinois.

————. 1993. "Whither Student Personnel Work from 1968 to 2018? A 1993 Retrospective." *NASPA Journal* 30: 162–68.

Shay, John E., Jr. Fall 1984. "Point of View. The Chief Student Affairs Officer and the President: Revisiting an Old Issue." *NASPA Journal* 22: 55–58.

Siegel, D.G. 14 March 1990. "Testimony before the Subcommittee on Postsecondary Education, House Committee on Education and Labor." *Hearings on H.R. 3344, The Crime Awareness and Campus Security Act of 1989.* Washington, D.C.: U.S. Congress.

Siggelkow, R.A. 1991. "Racism in Higher Education: A Permanent Condition?" *NASPA Journal* 28: 98–104.

Silverman, R.J. 1971. "The Student Personnel Worker on the Boundary." *Journal of College Student Personnel* 12: 3–6.

————. 1980. "The Student Personnel Administrator as Leading Edge Leader." *NASPA Journal* 18: 10–15.

Simpson, William Brand. 1991. *Cost Containment for Higher Education: Strategies for Public Policy and Institutional Administration.* New York: Praeger.

Smith, Daryl G. 1982. "The Next Step beyond Student Development: Becoming Partners within Our Institutions." *NASPA Journal* 19: 53–62.

Solomon, Lewis C. 1989. "Traditional College-age Students." In *Shaping Higher Education's Future: Demographic Realities and Opportunities, 1990–2000,* edited by Arthur Levine and Associates. San Francisco: Jossey-Bass.

Sorochty, R.W. 1991. "Planning and Assessment Equal Accountability." *NASPA Journal* 28: 355–61.

Stage, F.K. 1989. "College Outcomes and Student Development: Filling the Gaps." *Review of Higher Education* 12: 293–304.

Stamatakos, L.C. 1981. "Student Affairs Progress toward Professionalism: Recommendations for Action. Part 1." *Journal of College Student Personnel* 22: 105–13.

————. 1991. "Student Affairs Administrators as Institutional Leaders." In *Administration and Leadership in Student Affairs: Actualizing Student Development in Higher Education,* edited by T.K. Miller, R.B. Winston, and Associates. 2d ed. Muncie, Ind.: Accelerated Development, Inc.

Stamatakos, L.C., and R. Rodgers. 1984. "Student Affairs: A Profession in Need of a Philosophy." *Journal of College Student Personnel* 28: 146–50.

Steltenpohl, Elizabeth, and Jane Shipton. 1986. "Facilitating a Successful Transition to College for Adults." *Journal of Higher Education* 57: 637–58.

Stern, Kelly R. 1992. "Regulations: Presidential Perceptions." *Educational Record* 73: 17–20.

Stewart, David W. 1991. "Immigration and Higher Education: The Crisis and the Opportunities." *Educational Record* 72: 4.

Stickel, Sue A., and Kathryn Ellis. 1991. "Dating Relationships of Entering Freshmen: A Baseline Study of Courtship Violence." Paper presented at an annual meeting of the American Educational Research Association, February 13–16, Boston, Massachusetts. ED 334 477. 12 pp. MF–01; PC–01.

Stodt, M.M. 1987a. "Educational Excellence as a Prescription for Retention." In *Increasing Retention: Academic and Student Affairs Administrators in Partnership,* edited by Martha M. Stodt and William M. Klopper. New Directions for Higher Education No. 60. San Francisco: Jossey-Bass.

————. 1987b. "Intentional Student Development and Retention." In *Increasing Retention: Academic and Student Affairs Administrators in Partnership,* edited by Martha M. Stodt and William M. Klopper. New Directions for Higher Education No. 60. San Francisco: Jossey-Bass.

Strange, C. 1983. "Human Development Theory and Administrative Practice in Student Affairs: Ships Passing in the Daylight?" *NASPA Journal* 21: 2–8.

Study Group on the Conditions of Excellence in American Higher Education. 1984. *Involvement in Learning: Realizing the Potential of American Higher Education.* Washington, D.C.: National Institute of Education. ED 246 833. 127 pp. MF–01; PC–06.

Suzuki, Bob H. 1989. "Asians." In *Shaping Higher Education's Future: Demographic Realities and Opportunities, 1990–2000,* edited by Arthur Levine and Associates. San Francisco: Jossey-Bass.

Thomas, Gail E., and Deborah J. Hirsch. 1989. "Blacks." In *Shaping Higher Education's Future: Demographic Realities and Opportunities, 1990–2000,* edited by Arthur Levine and Associates. San Francisco: Jossey-Bass.

Tinsley, D.J., and T.M. Irelan. 1989. "Instruments Used in College Student Affairs Research: An Analysis of the Measurement Base of a Young Profession." *Journal of College Student Development* 30: 440–47.

Tinto, V. 1987. *Leaving College: Rethinking the Causes and Cures of Student Attrition.* Chicago: Univ. of Chicago Press.

U.S. Commission on Civil Rights. 1990. *Bigotry and Violence on American College Campuses.* Washington, D.C.: Author. ED 327 627. 87 pp. MF–01; PC–04.

Upcraft, M. Lee, John N. Gardiner, and Associates. 1989. *The Freshman Year Experience.* San Francisco: Jossey-Bass.

Vaala, L.D. 1989. "Practical Theories for Student Affairs Administrators." *NASPA Journal* 27: 108–15.

Waggaman, John S. 1991. *Strategies and Consequences: Managing the Costs in Higher Education.* ASHE-ERIC Higher Education Report

No. 8. Washington, D.C.: George Washington Univ., School of Education and Human Development. ED 347 921. 148 pp. MF–01; PC–06.

Watkins, B.T. 1992. "Scholars Are Urged to Collaborate in Today's Technology Revolution." *Chronicle of Higher Education* 39(10): A25.

Webb, E.M. 1987. "Retention and Excellence through Student Involvement: A Leadership Role for Student Affairs." *NASPA Journal* 24: 6–11.

Weidman, J. 1989. "Undergraduate Socialization: A Conceptual Approach." In *Higher Education: Handbook of Theory and Research,* vol. 5, edited by John Smart. New York: Agathon.

Wing, Sue D., P. Arredondo, and R.J. McDavis. 1992. "Multicultural Counseling Competencies and Standards: A Call to the Profession." *Journal of Counseling and Development* 70: 477–87.

Winston, Gordon C. 1992. "Hostility, Maximization, and the Public Trust." *Change* 24: 4.

Wolfe, Janice S. 1993. "Institutional Integration, Academic Success, and Persistence of First-year Commuter and Resident Students." *Journal of College Student Development* 34: 321–26.

Wood, L., R.B. Winston, and M.C. Polkosnik. 1985. "Career Orientations and Professional Development of Young Student Affairs Professionals." *Journal of College Student Personnel* 26: 532–39.

Wood, S.A. 1991. "Toward Renewed Collegiality: The Challenge of the 1990s." *NASPA Journal* 29: 2–9.

Woodard, Dudley B., Jr., R. Hyman, M.Von Destinon, and A. Jamison. 1991. "Student Affairs and Outcomes Assessment: A National Survey." *NASPA Journal* 29: 16–23.

Woodard, Dudley B., Jr., and Susan R. Komives. 1990. "Ensuring Staff Competence." In *New Futures for Student Affairs,* edited by Margaret Barr, M. Lee Upcraft, and Associates. San Francisco: Jossey-Bass.

Wrenn, C.G. 1968. "The Development of Student Personnel Work in the United States and Some Guidelines for the Future." In *The Student and the System,* edited by M.J. Minter. Boulder, Colo.: Western Interstate Commission on Higher Education.

Wright, D.J. 1987. "Responding to the Needs of Today's Minority Students." New Directions for Student Services No. 38. San Francisco: Jossey-Bass.

Wright, Loyd S., W. David Watts, and John Garrison. 1993. "A Strategy for Combining Elements of Alcohol–Drug and HIV–AIDS Prevention Programs on College Campuses." *NASPA Journal* 30: 298–308.

Zemsky, Robert, and William F. Massey. 1990. "Cost Containment: Committing to a New Economic Reality." *Change* 26: 16–22.

INDEX

A

13th Gen: Abort, Retry, Ignore, Fail?, 33
A Nation at Risk, 22
acquaintance rape, 15
administrative
        orientation professional, 55
        taxonomy, a collaborative, 71
        theory, reluctance to incorporate into role, 58
adult students, decline in, 12
African Americans
        campus experience attention paid to, 29
        likely to select colleges because of low tuition, 34
        matriculation decreases, 10
        participation rate in higher education, 28-29
        rate of growth varies per region, 12
alcohol, student use and abuse, 36
American College Personnel Association (ACPA), 6, 106
        Commission IX, 90
American Council on Education, 5, 83
Americans with Disabilities Act, 21, 30, 73
Asian-American
        areas of concentration, 12
        students, 10-11
Assessment, higher priority on campuses, 22
Assessment-Intervention of Student Problems (AISP) model, 74
Association of College Unions-International (ACU-I), 106

B

business careers, interest in declining, 35

C

California
        budget cuts in, 13
        Higher Education Policy Center, 34
        need expansion in higher education, 13
        youth will be more than 50% minority origin, 9-10
Campus
        and community programs, 64
        ecology managers. See mileu management
        Security Act, 21
CAS. See Council for the Advancement of Standards
Case Western Reserve University, xix
change generated opportunities, proactive toward, 54
Chickering, Arthur, 83
chief student affairs officer roles, 68
Civil War, 4, 59
classroom, experiences outside importance of, xvii
cognitive development model, 87

collaboration

        focal points between academic and student affairs, 62

        with other institutions and businesses, 50

collaborative problem solving

        learning skills, 99

        should foster, 103

college impact models, 87

college or university leader, qualities necessary, 67-68

Commission on National and Community Service, 99

Continuous Quality Improvement (CQI), 43

cost reduction principles, 49

Council for the Advancement of Standards (CAS), 94, 95

Council of Student Personnel Associations (COSPA) model, 85

court actions, influence on higher education, 24

D

dean of students, origin of position, xvii

demographic diversification of student body, 77

developmental theory, limits on use, 58

Drug-Free Schools and Communities Act, 100

drugs, high levels of use among upperclassmen, 36

dynamic tension on campus, greatest sources of today, 59-60

E

enrollment management, 46, 61

Elliot, Charles William, 4

ethnic studies courses, 77

European Common Market, 16

F

Feldman, Kenneth A., xvii, 83

Freedom Riders, 63-64

functional teams management, 61

funding decline, 23

G

Garland, Peter H., xvii

Generation X, 33

German university model, xvii

Grace, Thomas W., xvii

graduate programs requirements, 105-106

H

Harper, William Rainey, 82

Harvard, first personnel dean at, 4

hate crimes, 15

Hawaii, youth will be more than 50% minority origin, 9-10

Hendrickson, Robert, xix

Higher Education
        institutions central and defining goal, 2
        loss of public trust in, 19-20
        Reauthorization Act, 13, 21
HIV/AIDS
        and college students sexual behavior, 36-37
        epidemic, responding to, 99-100
How College Affects Students, xvii

I

India, 16
Indonesia, 16
information technology, continuing advances in, 44-45
        allows professionals to learn more about students &
            programs, 45
        increases capacity of student affairs organizations, 45
        makes possible need for fewer people, 45
Involvement in Learning, 22
institutional
        environment, assessment required, 103
        priority, development of the whole person, 6
Institutional changes in decade of 1990's, 1-2
        societal changes, 1
        changes in higher education, 1-2
        changes in students, 2
institutions, recommendations for, 105
Intentional Student Development and Retention Consortium, 47

K

Kohlberg, Lawrence, 83

L

Latino students, 10
        areas of concentration, 12
        campus experience attention paid to, 29

M

management
        in student affairs literature, 43
        of institutions, contribute to, 104-105
Maryland, budget cuts in, 13
Maryville College, xix
Mexico, 16
middle-class families, eroding ability to afford higher
    education, 16
mileu management, 56-58
minorities, numbers continue to increase, 9
minority faculty, increase of, 77

Moore, Leila, xix
Morgan, John, xix
multicultural campus
    critical phases in developing, 80
    fostering a, 100
multiculturalism on campus, 77-79

N

National Association of
    College Admissions Counselors (NACAC), 106
    Student Personnel Administrators (NASPA), 106
Native American students, 11
Nevada, high school graduates to increase, 12
New Jersey, budget cuts in, 13
New Perspectives for Student Affairs Professionals, xvii-xviii
New York University, xix, 73
New York, youth will be more than 50% minority origin, 9-10
new professionals, orientation and induction, 96-98
Newcomb, Theodore M., xvii, 83
North American Free Trade Agreement, 16

O

older students, types of will have important implications, 31-32
Oregon, budget cuts in, 13
Orrick, Helga, xix
outcomes research, 89

P

part-time students, increasing participation of, 29-30
Pascarella, E., xvii
Peace Corps members, 63-64
Pell grants, 13
Pennsylvania
    Department of Education, xix
    State University, xix
Perry, William, 83
person-environment theories, 86-87
Perspective on Student Affairs, 91
philosophy of life, student goal, 37
political activism on campus is reviving, 38
poorly prepared students, largest and fastest growing subgroup, 35
post-baby boomers, 33-34
private giving for higher education, 47-49
Process Model, 85
professional credibility with faculty, develop, 103-104
programs to reduce student attrition, 47
psychological research, 89
psychopathology, increasing levels on campus, 70, 72-75

psychosocial development model, 87

Q

quality management, 43-44
        principles, 69
quality of academic experience, contribute to, 104

R

research areas on student development, 89
revitalization strategies for institutions of higher education, 41-42
Right to Know Act, 21. See also Student Right to Know
Rutgers University, 73

S

Sanford, Nevit, 83
Sexual Assault Victims Bill of Rights, 100
sociological research, 89
student
        attrition, 75-76
        needs, disseminate information on, 104
        developmentalist perspective, 55
        disabilities, increasingly important group, 30-31
        of today, 27
        Personnel Point of View, 91
        Right to Know and Campus Security Act, 100
        services perspective, 55-56
student affairs profession
        "golden age", 5
        graduate programs in, 93-95
        integrative roles, 55-58
        peripheral to institution, 53
        recommendations for research in, 90
student affairs professionals
        as coordinator, 3-4
        as disciplinarian, 3
        as educator, 4-6
        as integrators within institutions, 7-8
        crime related challenges, 15
        evolution of role, 3
        preparation program model, 97
        recommendations for, 103-105
        revision of role of, 2
student development
        difficulties in using theories of, 81-82
        four elements of, 84
        movements significant for origin of, 82-83

substance
>abuse, dealing with, 100
>free zones, 73

T

technological sophistication, need for, 14
technology, applying new, 99
Terenzini, P.T., xvii
Texas, youth will be more than 50% minority origin, 9-10
The Impact of Colleges on Students, xvii
Tomorrow's Higher Education Project, 6
Total Quality Management (TQM), 43-44
tuition growth, 23

U

University of Chicago, 82
University of Michigan, 73
Upcraft, M. Lee, xix

V

violence on campus, addressing, 100
Virginia, budget cuts in, 13
Vista volunteers, 64

W

West Virginia, high school graduates to decrease, 11
When Dreams and Heroes Died, 38
women, represent increasing percentages of the college population, 27
World War I, 4, 82, 83
World War II, 5

ASHE-ERIC HIGHER EDUCATION REPORTS

Since 1983, the Association for the Study of Higher Education (ASHE) and the Educational Resources Information Center (ERIC) Clearinghouse on Higher Education, a sponsored project of the School of Education and Human Development at The George Washington University, have cosponsored the *ASHE-ERIC Higher Education Report* series. The 1993 series is the twenty-second overall and the fifth to be published by the School of Education and Human Development at the George Washington University.

Each monograph is the definitive analysis of a tough higher education problem, based on thorough research of pertinent literature and institutional experiences. Topics are identified by a national survey. Noted practitioners and scholars are then commissioned to write the reports, with experts providing critical reviews of each manuscript before publication.

Eight monographs (10 before 1985) in the ASHE-ERIC Higher Education Report series are published each year and are available on individual and subscription bases. Subscription to eight issues is $98.00 annually; $78 to members of AAHE, AIR, or AERA; and $68 to ASHE members. All foreign subscribers must include an additional $10 per series year for postage.

To order, use the order form on the last page of this book. Regular prices are as follows:

Series	Price	Series	Price
1993	$18.00	1985 to 87	$10.00
1990 to 92	$17.00	1983 and 84	$7.50
1988 and 89	$15.00	before 1983	$6.50

Discounts on non-subscription orders:
• Bookstores, and current members of AERA, AIR, AAHE and ASHE, receive a 25% discount.
• Bulk: For non-bookstore, non-member orders of 10 or more books, deduct 10%.

Shipping costs are as follows:
• U.S. address: 5% of invoice subtotal for orders over $50.00; $2.50 for each order with an invoice subtotal of $50.00 or less.
• Foreign: $2.50 per book.
   All orders under $45.00 must be prepaid. Make check payable to ASHE-ERIC. For Visa or MasterCard, include card number, expiration date and signature.

Address order to
   ASHE-ERIC Higher Education Reports
   The George Washington University
   1 Dupont Circle, Suite 630
   Washington, DC 20036
Or phone (202) 296-2597, toll-free: 800-773-ERIC.
   Write or call for a complete catalog.

1993 ASHE-ERIC Higher Education Reports

1. The Department Chair: New Roles, Responsibilities and Challenges
   Alan T. Seagren, John W. Creswell, and Daniel W. Wheeler

2. Sexual Harassment in Higher Education: From Conflict to Community
   Robert O. Riggs, Patricia H. Murrell, and JoAnn C. Cutting

3. Chicanos in Higher Education: Issues and Dilemmas for the 21st Century
   by Adalberto Aguirre, Jr., and Ruben O. Martinez

4. Academic Freedom in American Higher Education: Rights, Responsibilities, and Limitations
   by Robert K. Poch

5. Making Sense of the Dollars: The Costs and Uses of Faculty Compensation
   by Kathryn M. Moore and Marilyn J. Amey

6. Enhancing Promotion, Tenure and Beyond: Faculty Socialization as Cultural Process
   by William G. Tierney and Robert A. Rhoads

1992 ASHE-ERIC Higher Education Reports

1. The Leadership Compass: Values and Ethics in Higher Education
   John R. Wilcox and Susan L. Ebbs

2. Preparing for a Global Community: Achieving an International Perspective in Higher Education
   Sarah M. Pickert

3. Quality: Transforming Postsecondary Education
   Ellen Earle Chaffee and Lawrence A. Sherr

4. Faculty Job Satisfaction: Women and Minorities in Peril
   Martha Wingard Tack and Carol Logan Patitu

5. Reconciling Rights and Responsibilities of Colleges and Students: Offensive Speech, Assembly, Drug Testing, and Safety
   Annette Gibbs

6. Creating Distinctiveness: Lessons from Uncommon Colleges and Universities
   Barbara K. Townsend, L. Jackson Newell, and Michael D. Wiese

7. Instituting Enduring Innovations: Achieving Continuity of Change in Higher Education
   Barbara K. Curry

8. Crossing Pedagogical Oceans: International Teaching Assistants in U.S. Undergraduate Education
   Rosslyn M. Smith, Patricia Byrd, Gayle L. Nelson, Ralph Pat Barrett, and Janet C. Constantinides

1991 ASHE-ERIC Higher Education Reports

1. Active Learning: Creating Excitement in the Classroom
   Charles C. Bonwell and James A. Eison

2. Realizing Gender Equality in Higher Education: The Need to Integrate Work/Family Issues
   Nancy Hensel

3. Academic Advising for Student Success: A System of Shared Responsibility
   Susan H. Frost

4. Cooperative Learning: Increasing College Faculty Instructional Productivity
   David W. Johnson, Roger T. Johnson, and Karl A. Smith

5. High School–College Partnerships: Conceptual Models, Programs, and Issues
   Arthur Richard Greenberg

6. Meeting the Mandate: Renewing the College and Departmental Curriculum
   William Toombs and William Tierney

7. Faculty Collaboration: Enhancing the Quality of Scholarship and Teaching
   Ann E. Austin and Roger G. Baldwin

8. Strategies and Consequences: Managing the Costs in Higher Education
   John S. Waggaman

1990 ASHE-ERIC Higher Education Reports

1. The Campus Green: Fund Raising in Higher Education
   Barbara E. Brittingham and Thomas R. Pezzullo

2. The Emeritus Professor: Old Rank - New Meaning
   James E. Mauch, Jack W. Birch, and Jack Matthews

3. "High Risk" Students in Higher Education: Future Trends
   Dionne J. Jones and Betty Collier Watson

4. Budgeting for Higher Education at the State Level: Enigma, Paradox, and Ritual
   Daniel T. Layzell and Jan W. Lyddon

5. Proprietary Schools: Programs, Policies, and Prospects
   John B. Lee and Jamie P. Merisotis

---

6. College Choice: Understanding Student Enrollment Behavior
   Michael B. Paulsen

7. Pursuing Diversity: Recruiting College Minority Students
   Barbara Astone and Elsa Nuñez-Wormack

8. Social Consciousness and Career Awareness: Emerging Link
   in Higher Education
   John S. Swift, Jr.

1989 ASHE-ERIC Higher Education Reports

1. Making Sense of Administrative Leadership: The 'L' Word in
   Higher Education
   Estela M. Bensimon, Anna Neumann, and Robert Birnbaum

2. Affirmative Rhetoric, Negative Action: African-American and
   Hispanic Faculty at Predominantly White Universities
   Valora Washington and William Harvey

3. Postsecondary Developmental Programs: A Traditional Agenda
   with New Imperatives
   Louise M. Tomlinson

4. The Old College Try: Balancing Athletics and Academics in
   Higher Education
   John R. Thelin and Lawrence L. Wiseman

5. The Challenge of Diversity: Involvement or Alienation in the
   Academy?
   Daryl G. Smith

6. Student Goals for College and Courses: A Missing Link in Assessing and Improving Academic Achievement
   Joan S. Stark, Kathleen M. Shaw, and Malcolm A. Lowther

7. The Student as Commuter: Developing a Comprehensive Institutional Response
   Barbara Jacoby

8. Renewing Civic Capacity: Preparing College Students for Service
   and Citizenship
   Suzanne W. Morse

1988 ASHE-ERIC Higher Education Reports

1. The Invisible Tapestry: Culture in American Colleges and
   Universities
   George D. Kuh and Elizabeth J. Whitt

2. Critical Thinking: Theory, Research, Practice, and Possibilities
   Joanne Gainen Kurfiss

3. Developing Academic Programs: The Climate for Innovation
   Daniel T. Seymour

4. Peer Teaching: To Teach is To Learn Twice
   Neal A. Whitman

5. Higher Education and State Governments: Renewed Partnership,
   Cooperation, or Competition?
   Edward R. Hines

6. Entrepreneurship and Higher Education: Lessons for Colleges,
   Universities, and Industry
   James S. Fairweather

7. Planning for Microcomputers in Higher Education: Strategies
   for the Next Generation
   *Reynolds Ferrante, John Hayman, Mary Susan Carlson, and
   Harry Phillips*

8. The Challenge for Research in Higher Education: Harmonizing
   Excellence and Utility
   Alan W. Lindsay and Ruth T. Neumann

1987 ASHE-ERIC Higher Education Reports

1. Incentive Early Retirement Programs for Faculty: Innovative
   Responses to a Changing Environment
   Jay L. Chronister and Thomas R. Kepple, Jr.

2. Working Effectively with Trustees: Building Cooperative Campus
   Leadership
   Barbara E. Taylor

3. Formal Recognition of Employer-Sponsored Instruction: Conflict
   and Collegiality in Postsecondary Education
   Nancy S. Nash and Elizabeth M. Hawthorne

4. Learning Styles: Implications for Improving Educational Practices
   Charles S. Claxton and Patricia H. Murrell

5. Higher Education Leadership: Enhancing Skills through Professional Development Programs
   Sharon A. McDade

6. Higher Education and the Public Trust: Improving Stature in
   Colleges and Universities
   Richard L. Alfred and Julie Weissman

7. College Student Outcomes Assessment: A Talent Development
   Perspective
   Maryann Jacobi, Alexander Astin, and Frank Ayala, Jr.

8. Opportunity from Strength: Strategic Planning Clarified with
   Case Examples
   Robert G. Cope

1986 ASHE-ERIC Higher Education Reports

1. Post-tenure Faculty Evaluation: Threat or Opportunity?
   Christine M. Licata

2. Blue Ribbon Commissions and Higher Education: Changing Academe from the Outside
   Janet R. Johnson and Laurence R. Marcus

3. Responsive Professional Education: Balancing Outcomes and Opportunities
   Joan S. Stark, Malcolm A. Lowther, and Bonnie M.K. Hagerty

4. Increasing Students' Learning: A Faculty Guide to Reducing Stress among Students
   Neal A. Whitman, David C. Spendlove, and Claire H. Clark

5. Student Financial Aid and Women: Equity Dilemma?
   Mary Moran

6. The Master's Degree: Tradition, Diversity, Innovation
   Judith S. Glazer

7. The College, the Constitution, and the Consumer Student: Implications for Policy and Practice
   Robert M. Hendrickson and Annette Gibbs

8. Selecting College and University Personnel: The Quest and the Question
   Richard A. Kaplowitz

*Out-of-print. Available through EDRS. Call 1-800-443-ERIC.

Quantity		Amount
_____	Please begin my subscription to the 1993 *ASHE-ERIC Higher Education Reports* at $98.00, 32% off the cover price, starting with Report 1, 1993.	_____
_____	Please send a complete set of the 1992 *ASHE-ERIC Higher Education Reports* at $90.00, 33% off the cover price.	_____
_____	Outside the U.S., add $10.00 per series for postage.	_____

Individual reports are avilable at the following prices:

1993, $18.00	1985 to 1987, $10.00
1990 to 1992, $17.00	1983 and 1984, $7.50
1988 and 1989, $15.00	1980 to 1982, $6.50

SHIPPING: **U.S. Orders:** *For subtotal (before discount) of $50.00 or less, add $2.50. For subtotal over $50.00, add 5% of subtotal. Call for rush service options.* **Foreign Orders:** *$2.50 per book.* **U.S. Subscriptions:** *Included in price.* **Foreign Subscriptions:** *Add $10.00.*

PLEASE SEND ME THE FOLLOWING REPORTS:

Quantity	Report No.	Year	Title	Amount

Subtotal:	
Shipping:	
Total Due:	

Please check one of the following:
- ☐ Check enclosed, payable to GWU–ERIC.
- ☐ Purchase order attached ($45.00 minimum).
- ☐ Charge my credit card indicated below:
  - ☐ Visa   ☐ MasterCard

Expiration Date _____

Name _____

Title _____

Institution _____

Address _____

City _____ State _____ Zip _____

Phone _____ Fax _____ Telex _____

Signature _____ Date _____

SEND ALL ORDERS TO:
ASHE-ERIC Higher Education Reports
The George Washington University
One Dupont Circle, Suite 630
Washington, DC 20036-1183
Phone: (202) 296-2597
Toll-free: 800-773-ERIC

Cooking Well

Fibromyalgia

Marie-Annick Courtier

Foreword by Lauren Feder, M.D.

Acknowledgments

Hatherleigh Press would like to extend a special thank you to June Eding—without your hard work and dedication this book would not have been possible.

trigger other problems. For example, pain caused by fibromyalgia can lead to depression and/or sleep deprivation, which may, in turn, make an individual even more susceptible to pain. It is important that fibromyalgia sufferers make lifestyle changes to reduce as many symptoms as possible so that one condition does not lead to or exacerbate another.

Causes

Fibromyalgia is most common among women, with 75-90% of fibromyalgia patients being female. But the condition can strike anyone; it also afflicts men and children, and occurs across all ethnic groups. Those at highest risk for fibromyalgia include people whose family members have had the condition. Additionally, 20–30% of individuals with rheumatoid arthritis and systemic lupus erythematosus may also have fibromyalgia. Some fibromyalgia patients experience a slow onset of the disease but for most, the condition is triggered by an illness or injury. In these cases, the illness or injury doesn't necessarily cause fibromyalgia, but reveals a condition already present in the body for some time.

Currently, the cause of fibromyalgia is unknown. There are several theories as to what may cause fibromyalgia, but the leading hypothesis concerns *central sensitization*. This theory states that people with fibromyalgia have a lower tolerance for pain due to increased sensitivity in the brain and pain signals. This theorizes that fibromyalgia is a disorder of the central nervous system.

Other potential causes of the disease include:

- Low levels of blood flow to the thalamus region of the brain

- Low levels of serotonin and tryptophan

- Stress-related disorders such as chronic fatigue syndrome, depression, and irritable bowel syndrome often occur at the same time as fibromyalgia. This has lead many doctors to theorize that stress may play a role in causing fibromyalgia.

Treatment

There is currently no cure for fibromyalgia. However, a multi-tiered approach, carefully catered to each individual's needs, is effective at lowering the incidence of symptoms.

Often the most pressing concern for those with fibromyalgia is pain

Chapter 1

Living with Fibromyalgia

Fibromyalgia is a chronic pain condition that affects approximately 10 million people in the United States alone and an estimated 4% of individuals worldwide.

Fibromyalgia (also known as FM or FMS) is classified as a medical disorder and is characterized by chronic, widespread pain. The word fibromyalgia literally means "tissue or muscle pain" ("fibro" means fibrous tissue, "myo" means muscle, and "algia" means pain).

Those with fibromyalgia often experience pain as a constant, dull ache throughout the body, although it may be felt more often in or around the neck, shoulders, upper chest, elbows, hips, and knees. Fibromyalgia also causes extreme sensitivity to pressure (known as *allodynia*).

Because those with fibromyalgia suffer from many other symptoms in addition to pain, the disorder is also referred to as "fibromyalgia syndrome" to better describe the wide variety of effects caused throughout the body by this condition.

Fibromyalgia may cause:
- Tingling of the skin and muscle spasms
- Restless leg syndrome
- Fatigue and sleep disturbances
- Chronic fatigue syndrome
- Anxiety and/or depression
- Headaches and/or dizziness
- Irritable bowel syndrome
- Impaired memory and concentration

Many of these symptoms, if not addressed, can make conditions worse or

Foreword

Cooking Well: Fibromyalgia comes at a timely period, as fibromyalgia (FM) currently afflicts millions of Americans. Because FM can involve many different organ systems in the body, its effects on patients—as well as their families and friends—cannot be overstated. Despite the medical advancements in the 21st century, there are limited resources in the standard health care field with regards to FM, and patients and doctors are becoming more interested in finding ways to improve quality of life and health that go beyond medication. One effective approach is to follow a healthy diet, and *Cooking Well: Fibromyalgia* shows readers exactly how to do this.

In addition to presenting delicious healthy recipes, the first part of this book provides an excellent description about fibromyalgia syndrome with easy-to-understand scientific and medical information. As a holistic physician, I appreciate the whole-health approach in describing how diet, lifestyle, exercise, attitude, and rest become important components in the road to feeling better and enjoying improved energy for those with FM.

Now, more than ever, people are interested in partnering with their healthcare practitioners and taking a proactive role in their healthcare. Coupled with the idea that more doctors are beginning to recognize the importance of healthy nutrition for FM, *Cooking Well: Fibromyalgia* offers readers an innovative concept that food is one of our best medicines. Hippocrates wrote, "Let food be your medicine and medicine be your food". The fact that organic foods and farmers markets are becoming more commonplace in our cities is an indication that people are interested in consuming the best foods for optimal health.

As a cookbook, the following recipes are appealing to both the novice cook and the gourmet chef, and can be used as a guide on how to eat right and make healthier choices on a daily basis. *Cooking Well: Fibromyalgia* offers sound advice to all palates and is appropriate for partners and families as well. This book has greatly expanded my opportunity as a physician to counsel my patients regarding fibromyalgia and the connection to a healthier diet. *Cooking Well: Fibromyalgia* is an important book for people with FM as well as their healthcare practitioners.

—*Lauren Feder, M.D.*

Table of Contents

management. A doctor will work with the patient to develop a plan to minimize pain, which can include prescription drugs (currently, the most frequently prescribed include pregabalin, duloxetine and milnacipran). In some cases, localized injections can be administered to specific sites that are causing extreme pain.

In addition to partnering with a doctor to develop guidelines for medical care, making healthy lifestyle choices in the areas of nutrition, stress management, and exercise are vital. Along with eating well and reducing stress, many alternative medical and lifestyle approaches (such as acupuncture, meditation, and yoga) can also be beneficial to those with fibromyalgia.

Leading a Healthy Life

As discussed earlier, because some fibromyalgia symptoms can further exacerbate others, treating fibromyalgia effectively is of the utmost importance—and a treatment program must go beyond simply taking medicine or seeing a doctor. Patients with fibromyalgia must commit to leading healthy lives in order to feel better, and this includes building positive daily and long-term habits.

Getting enough rest is key. Those with fibromyalgia should be sure to set aside enough time to sleep and develop good sleeping habits. Avoiding napping if possible, so that it is easier to go to bed and wake up at the same time, can also be helpful.

Another important issue for those with fibromyalgia is the management of stress. Anyone with the condition should be sure to reduce stress in his or her life and, to the extent possible, limit overexertion and emotional distress because extreme stress can agitate the symptoms of fibromyalgia. It's important to remember that reducing stress does not mean becoming inactive. Minimizing stress doesn't mean you have to quit your job or stop doing the things you love. It merely means learning to manage stress better.

Exercising regularly is another key component to managing fibromyalgia symptoms. Because fibromyalgia often affects the joints and surrounding tissues, any exercise that will help to gently stretch the muscles and ligaments can help to relieve or prevent pain. Yoga, meditation, and other exercises that incorporate breathing into physical practice can also provide useful tools for managing stress while invigorating the body. Always consult your doctor before beginning any exercise routine. Choose an exercise that raises the heart rate but does not trigger joint pain. Start out with exercises that reduce stress on the joints.

Some good exercises include:

- Walking
- Swimming
- Water aerobics
- Biking
- Stretching

When beginning any exercise program, fibromyalgia patients should be sure to pace themselves and start slow. If it becomes a problem to find time to exercise regularly, efforts should be made to keep active in other ways. This can be as simple as walking an extra block or parking a bit further from a store's entrance to get a little more exercise on the way to the door. A good rule for those with fibromyalgia to keep in mind is, "if you have the energy to do things, use it, but be careful not to overexert yourself."

Another necessary component to maintaining a healthy lifestyle is eating well. In the next chapter we will take a closer look at how making the right food choices can reduce the severity of symptoms and improve the quality of living for those with fibromyalgia.

Chapter 2

How the Right Diet Can Help

Although there is no dietary "cure" for fibromyalgia, eating well can make a major difference for those living with the condition. Choosing the right foods and avoiding the wrong ones can help to make you feel better and improve daily functioning. The benefits of eating the right foods go a long way; they include boosting overall energy and improving the immune system, in addition to potentially lessening or even eliminating the severity of symptoms. Eating delicious, fresh fruits and vegetables not only provides the body with the nutrients it needs, but also elevates mood and overall physical performance. Following a diet rich in key ingredients will improve your well-being, no matter what your symptoms.

Making the Right Choices

Just as the right diet can help, the wrong foods can worsen the symptoms of fibromyalgia. Follow the guidelines in this book when formulating a meal plan for yourself to be sure you are not eating anything that will set you back on the road to health.

Keep in mind that each individual is different and that while some foods may not bother certain individuals, others will prefer to stay away from anything that causes them discomfort or worsens their symptoms. Of course, those with any specific food allergies should avoid problem foods altogether.

Speak to your doctor about the dietary guidelines below and seek his or her guidance based on your own unique symptoms and needs before beginning any eating regimen.

Basic Nutrition

If you have not already, eliminate the most bothersome foods and habits, as listed below, from your diet. Many fibromyalgia patients report that cutting out harmful foods makes a major difference in how they feel. Let these changes be your first step towards health:

- **REMOVE artificial ingredients, additives, and chemicals from your regular diet. This includes cutting out processed foods, preservatives, chemicals, and artificial sweeteners.**
  The presence of artificial products can cause stress to our bodies on a cellular level, known as *oxidative stress*. Oxidative stress occurs when the body manufactures chemicals knows as *free radicals*, which are produced in response to the presence of artificial chemicals in the body. Higher oxidative stress may lead to lower pain thresholds, more muscle pain, and increased fatigue. In particular, artificial sweeteners have been linked to increased fibromyalgia symptoms (you can also combat oxidative stress by eating more antioxidants, see page 7).
- **AVOID fried, fatty, highly caloric, and processed foods.**
- **ALSO AVOID refined sugar, caffeine, alcohol, junk/fast food, unnecessary drugs, non-organic foods, and any other foods high in sugar, fat, and cholesterol.**

Keep in mind that eliminating any products that you are accustomed to using will take time. If you would like to cut something out of your diet for good, be sure to avoid it for at least a month. This will reduce your cravings and make the habit easier to maintain over the long term. Some individuals report feeling better after removing specific items from their diet entirely. If you like, try eliminating all forms of caffeine, fried, processed and fatty foods for a month. This will help you to find out if eating these specific things may have been contributing to your symptoms.

As you cut down on bad habits, work to make improvements, too. Follow these basic guidelines:

- **Increase Choice:** Eat a wide variety of foods in a variety of amounts and combinations. By eating this way, you are more likely to consume all the vitamins, minerals and fatty acids that your body needs on a daily basis.

- **Eat Organic:** Avoid any vegetables, fruits and meats that are artificially produced with pesticides, fertilizers, or other chemicals. Seek to eat fruits and vegetables that are as fresh as possible to ensure that you are getting the most vitamins and nutritional value (more on organic foods in the next chapter).

- **Eat Often:** It is best to eat small meals throughout the day. Enjoy a light meal as often as every four hours to keep your metabolism moving and your energy up.

- **Be Balanced:** Balance the consumption of lean animal and vegetable proteins with complex carbohydrates, healthy plant fats, and essential fatty acids (more on the definition of these food categories in the following chapters).

- **Drink Water:** Drink 8-10 glasses of purified water each day.

Dietary Suggestions

Specific foods can especially help fibromyalgia patients. In addition to following the basic guidelines listed above, seek out these helpful foods:

Eat foods high in lean protein. This is key for maintaining the health of muscle fibers, which need protein to repair lost muscle tissue.

Seek out foods high in antioxidants. Many of the recipes in this book feature fruits and vegetables that are packed with antioxidants. This is because antioxidants work to minimize oxidative stress and possibly prevent increased levels of pain and fatigue.

Foods high in antioxidants that may be beneficial for those with fibromyalgia include:
- Red kidney beans
- Pinto beans
- Black beans
- Blueberries
- Cranberries

- Blackberries
- Raspberries
- Strawberries
- Apples (including Red Delicious, Gala and Granny Smith)
- Cherries
- Black plums
- Russet potatoes
- Artichokes
- Dried prunes
- Walnuts
- Cashews
- Pistachios
- Almonds

Fruits, vegetables, whole grains, and dairy products are all good sources of nutrients for those living with fibromyalgia. When using dairy products, seek out those that are low in fat.

Leafy green vegetables are a good source of calcium. Boost your consumption of leafy greens if you are seeking to reduce your dairy intake (or if you are allergic to dairy) to ensure you get all the calcium your body needs.

Be sure to include good fats in your diet that can come from foods like raw nuts, vegetable oils, flaxseeds, flaxseed oil, and avocado.

Making a Change

Eating well can make a big difference in how you feel. But change doesn't happen overnight. How should you begin to ensure long-term success?

The best way to begin any task is to learn what steps lie ahead of you. Look within. The first step towards implementing lifelong change is to be aware of your body. This is especially important for those with fibromyalgia, who face the challenges of pain management on a daily basis.

Begin keeping a journal. Start to think carefully about how pain has affected you. Consider what occurred yesterday, or the week prior. Try to recall specifics about the times you felt well; and when you started not to feel well. As time goes by, you can review your journal to see what you did in the last hour, twenty-four hours, and forty-eight hours: what you ate, what you drank, if you ate out, if you over-exercised, did not exercise, worked too hard, or skipped or changed your medicine. All this will give you clues as to what may have triggered painful symptoms.

You might not discover right away the possible reasons for added pain or stress. You need to show patience, as it may take awhile. A positive attitude and strong will are extremely important.

Sometimes the cause may be more than just physical. Is it possible that an emotional event (for example divorce, or loss of someone) or a stressful situation triggered the problem? Is a situation making you irritable or frustrated? Are you anxious about a situation, such as moving? Remember, reducing levels of stress is one of the most important tasks for those with fibromyalgia. Keeping a journal and reviewing what upset your regular routine and increased your painful symptoms is a great first step.

Once you figure out your possible triggers, make sure you watch out for those situations in order to avoid repeating them. If you know a specific event or task causes you stress, work with others to make the circumstances more manageable for you or learn specific techniques for stress management (such as meditation and breathing awareness) to help you get through the event next time.

Lasting Change

Read and educate yourself as much as possible about fibromyalgia. Learn what lifestyle and food habits might help to lessen symptoms. Revise your strategies, goals, and any notes accordingly. Continue to try new things, little by little. If others have benefitted from a specific food, see if that works for you as well. Begin to establish a plan for a healthier lifestyle. Keep in mind what you have learned from your journal as you create your work schedule, as well as your exercise and meal routines, for the weeks and months ahead. Preparation will help you to keep your stress level low and improve your overall health to prevent further symptoms from flaring up. Remember, your goal is not only to reduce as many of your symptoms as possible, but to also stay positive so that you can enjoy your life.

When it comes to eating, keep in mind that, if you avoid certain foods due to intolerances or allergies, you may be depriving your body of major nutrients. This could be another reason you do not feel well. Consult your registered dietitian or nutritionist to find out if you need to take vitamin and/ or mineral supplements.

Reaching Out to Others

Be sure to remember that those around you are an important component of a healthy, meaningful life. Work on maintaining strong relationships with those closest to you. It is vital that you let your caregivers, helpers, colleagues, friends and family members know you need their support for the long run. Those who support you will help provide a source of strength when you have difficult days where your symptoms flare up.

If you haven't already, talk to your family and friends. Take time to explain your condition to them. Answer any questions they may have, and explain to them how fibromyalgia and its symptoms may effect your mood or day-to-day interactions. Do not feel intimidated about telling them about how specific fibromyalgia symptoms are affecting you. Remember: they are your friends and family. They love you and they will understand that some days may be better than others for you.

If they have further questions or want to help out in a specific way, you can even give them a copy of this book and explain that the recipes feature ingredients that are especially important for your condition. Tell them it will mean a great deal if you could cook some of these meals together. Teaming up can be fun, as well as helpful to you. Friends and family can help to make tasks easier for you on difficult days. For example, they can help out with food preparation or clean up so you can undertake the task of cooking. The reward will be sharing a memorable meal together.

No matter what activities you choose to do together, remember to thank those closest to you for their understanding and kindness. When you are feeling well, you can even write your own cookbook with the foods that make you feel best and share it with your friends. You can express your gratitude by including notes about meals you've shared. The comfort and kindness of a friend can go a long way and should be appreciated and treasured.

A Special Note

As you begin to implement changes in your life, be aware that psychological and physical stress often results in fatigue. Those with fibromyalgia should strive to be aware of how much energy they have available so they don't stress themselves further and worsen symptoms. Learn to help yourself through difficult times of stress through relaxation techniques such as meditation, massage therapy, and yoga. If you find yourself with some free time, be sure to take advantage of it. Whatever your favorite activity may be, from reading to taking a refreshing bath, don't hesitate to indulge yourself on a regular basis. Learning to care for yourself is imperative for your long-term health.

Chapter 3

Dietary Suggestions for a Healthy Lifestyle

No matter what your health problems, eating healthy foods should be a priority. You need to be responsible for your own health; don't expect anyone to keep you in line. As a matter of fact, many people will offer you foods that are not good for you. It is ultimately up to you to stay on track with your eating goals and say, "no thank you". Always pay attention to your nutrition plan and do everything in your power to stay as close to it as possible.

Keep in mind that you may slip up—this is understandable. Eating habits are difficult to change and are often rooted in years of cultural and family habits. Expecting a quick change is not realistic. Patience and a strong will to change over time are a must.

Healthy eating is not about eating everything you like. It is about giving your body what it needs and what agrees with it. It is about eating the right amount of calories per day considering your daily activities. Eating healthy is also about meal rituals. That means having regular meals at the same times every day. Three to four meals a day is recommended. This includes a snack in the afternoon, which is important to keep your blood sugar level stable if you have a late dinner. It is ultimately up to you to decide what works best for your body and how to spread your meals throughout your day. Remember to appropriately divide your daily calories.

Remember that eating should be a pleasant experience, too. Fresh fruits and vegetables and lean meats, when eaten plain or in a delicious recipe, can brighten your day. You will feel much better knowing that your food choices are enriching your life and possibly helping to reduce painful symptoms. By employing new habits, you will eventually see the fruits of your labor in an improved overall well-being.

Eating Organic

Everyone knows that eating foods that are free of pesticides, chemicals, antibiotics, colorings, or hormones is better for you. This is strongly recommended for those with fibromyalgia. If you are not financially strained, make an effort to shop organic at your local farmers' market, growers, and stores. If budget is an issue, do not stress about it. Sometimes we have to make practical decisions and, understandably, eating organic may not always be a priority. Also, keep in mind that due to very strict regulations, many farmers and growers are not able to obtain the organic label but are still producing foods that are free of pesticides, chemicals, antibiotics, and hormones, and are of excellent quality. All you need to do is find those products in your local stores and read their labels carefully.

Below are some buying tips that are economically prudent while also being healthier for you and your family.

- **When buying dry, canned, or frozen products you should make sure to buy organic.** They are not much more expensive and are much healthier for you. While you should not be eating such products on a regular basis, they can be helpful during the winter months, when a variety of vegetables and fruits are not available. Also, if you cook for yourself and feel physically exhausted, you might opt for the dry, canned or frozen product.

- **Reduce your individual portions, particularly with meat products.** You can stretch your dollars while you shrink your waistline. Portion sizes at your local store are often larger than what you really need to eat. For example, a chicken breast often weighs 8 ounces when you should only be eating about 4 ounces.

- **Support your local farmers and growers.** The more distance the food travels from farm to table, the greater the cost. Join a food co-op. Co-ops purchase food in bulk and often carry organic items. If there isn't one in your town, consider starting one with family and friends.

- **Share your knowledge.** If you have discovered healthy organic or non-organic foods from a reputable supplier, pass the news on via an e-mail to fibromyalgia organizations and friends. They will appreciate it immensely and you will help promote such suppliers, which eventually will be in a better position to lower prices based on demand.

Eating Out

Preferably, you should eat out no more than twice a week. Keep that time for the weekend with family and friends. Too many restaurants use commercially packaged food and unhealthy fats, which are detrimental to your health. Not to mention how much salt is in those foods! It is extremely important that you pay attention to the type of foods you choose when going out.

In a restaurant, do not hesitate to question the waiter about the ingredients in a particular dish. Let him/her know you are on a specific diet and looking for nutrient-rich dishes that are also low in fat. More and more chefs are willing to accommodate their clients today because they know it is important for the survival of the restaurant. There is also an increased demand for healthier choices, and the industry is paying attention. Choosing a restaurant that caters to foods closer to your diet is also wise—chances are you will find more food that you can enjoy there in the first place (e.g. Italian, Mediterranean, or vegetarian restaurants).

When visiting with family or friends, make them aware of your health situation a few days before the visit. If they already know, just give them a quick phone call to remind them, as many people have a very active lifestyle and may easily forget. Be very diligent and carefully choose what you eat. If needed, ask the host if he or she made the food from scratch, what is in it, or if it is store bought food. And remember: when in doubt, do not eat it. If you are not sure of the situation, you can always eat before you go to an event. If you know that the food the host will prepare will not agree with you, ask if you can bring your own food. No one should get upset; after all it is about making sure everyone enjoys the party!

While traveling, keep the same attitude that you have when you are eating out close to home. Be even more vigilant. It is best to bring your own food, but sometimes this is not possible (such as when traveling by airplane). When booking your flight, most airlines will gladly reserve a low-fat meal for you. Vegetarian meals may also be a good choice, but use caution as they are often based on cheese and carbohydrates. Ask specifically what foods are included in the meals. At the airport, look for food that is freshly prepared in front of you and as close as possible to your nutritional plan. Take with you enough snack foods to last you a day or two in case of schedule delays. Nuts, raisins, and dates are easy to carry. You will be able to find bottles of water, milk, or juice in most places.

When traveling abroad, be even more careful than you would be at home. Foods are not prepared the same way and many unknown ingredients may be a real problem to your health. Stick with plain grilled, steamed, broiled, or baked main courses with rice, potatoes, or steamed vegetables as side dishes. If you have no choice, pick the healthiest option and eat what you know is safe for you. Be careful with raw foods, as sanitation may not be as thorough as at home. Always ask for a bottle of water to be opened in front of you. Don't miss the opportunity to go to a local market and purchase some fresh fruits, vegetables, and healthy snacks such as almonds, walnuts, hazelnuts, dates, or whatever you may be able to keep in your hotel room.

Don't forget to wash the vegetables and fruits with a bottle of water mixed with a little vinegar. This will help kill bacteria not visible to the eye. If you have a refrigerator in the room, stock it with milk, yogurt, or cheese to provide you with low-fat sources of calcium and protein. Read all food labels carefully. If you don't understand the language, this may be a problem. See if the concierge or a person speaking your language at the hotel can assist you. Be on your guard at all times. If you take supplements or specific medications, make sure you have enough for your trip, plus a week's worth as back-up. Standards overseas are not always the same as in the United States.

Quick Tips for Ordering at a Restaurant

• Order steamed vegetables with olive oil or lemon on the side

• Brown rice is also safe

• Ask for your dish to be prepared with a little olive oil, canola oil, or grapeseed oil, and no butter. Ask for olive oil and vinegar on the side for your salad dressing or bring your own dressing. Half a lemon is also a good substitute for dressing or butter on steamed vegetables.

• Half a baked potato is safe as long as it is without toppings and butter (you can always drizzle a little olive oil over it yourself).

• Stay away from unhealthy carbohydrates and ask to substitute steamed vegetables instead. Avoid most desserts except fresh fruits. It is best to save your sweet tooth for homemade, healthier goodies that feature abundant amounts of fresh fruit.

• Don't blindly eat what is served to you—pay attention to the type of food and the amount of food, and try to figure out the total calories. Put that into perspective with your meal allowance.

Chapter 4

The Recipes

Breakfast

Granola with Banana, Apple, and Walnut

serves 2

ingredients

½ cup granola
½ cup low-fat milk
¼ small banana, peeled and sliced
¼ medium apple, peeled, cored, and diced
1 teaspoon chopped walnuts

cooking instructions

Mix the granola with the milk. Add the banana, apples, and walnuts, and serve immediately.

Kasha with Apples and Cinnamon

serves 1

ingredients

⅔ cup low-fat milk
(cow's, rice, soy, or nut)
2 tablespoons buckwheat groats
¼ teaspoon cinnamon
½ apple, diced

1 tablespoon raisins
1 teaspoon freshly ground
flaxseed
1 tablespoon honey
Pinch of salt

cooking instructions

In a saucepan, bring the milk to boil. Add the buckwheat groats, cinnamon, and salt. Mix and bring to boil. Reduce heat and simmer for 10 to 12 minutes.

Transfer to a serving bowl. Top with the diced apple, raisins, and flaxseeds. Drizzle honey and serve immediately.

Oatmeal with Kiwi and Banana

serves 1

✓ *Option:*
Add 1 teaspoon
flaxseed

ingredients

½ cup to ¾ cup oatmeal
1 cup to 1½ cups low-fat milk, hot
1 teaspoon almonds
1 kiwi, diced
½ banana, diced

cooking instructions

Mix the oatmeal with the hot milk until the liquid is incorporated. Add in the almonds, kiwi, banana, and serve immediately.

Cream of Millet

serves 1

ingredients

1 cup low-fat soy milk
(or low-fat milk)
1 teaspoon pumpkin pie spices
(optional)
¼ cup pearl millet
2 teaspoons slivered almonds
2 teaspoons maple syrup

½ peach, peeled, seeded,
and diced
1 teaspoon flaxseed oil
Small pinch of salt

✔ *If you use less cooking liquid, the millet grain is fluffier and crunchier. Try it with ¾ cup of the soy milk instead of the 1 cup used in the recipe. Using more liquid creates a more moist, soft texture. This is all about personal preference, so experiment and find the texture you like.*

Substitute the peach with apricot, apple, or mango.

cooking instructions

Warm the milk, salt, and pumpkin pie spices over medium heat in a small saucepan. Wash the millet a couple of times and drain well. Place the millet in another pan over medium heat. Add the almonds and the warm flavored soy milk. Reduce heat and simmer for 20 minutes or until all the liquid is absorbed.

Transfer to a serving bowl and mix in the maple syrup. Top with the fruits, drizzle flaxseed oil, and serve immediately.

All-Bran with Apples and Cinnamon

serves 1

ingredients

1 cup all bran flakes
½ cup low-fat milk
¼ cup apples
1 tablespoon raisins
1 teaspoon freshly ground flaxseeds
Cinnamon to taste (optional)

> ✓ *You may substitute low-fat milk with low-fat soy milk, low-fat rice milk, or low-fat almond milk.*

cooking instructions

In a bowl mix the cereal with the milk. Top with the apples, raisins, and flaxseeds. Sprinkle with cinnamon and serve immediately.

Wheat Bran Flakes with Berries and Raisins

serves 1

ingredients

1 cup wheat bran flakes
½ cup low-fat milk
¼ cup mixed fresh berries
1 tablespoon raisins
1 teaspoon flaxseeds

cooking instructions

In a bowl, mix the cereal with the milk. Top with the berries, raisins, and flaxseeds, and serve immediately.

Muesli with Dried Fruit and Nuts
serves 1

ingredients
½ cup muesli cereal
½ cup low-fat plain yogurt
Milk (optional)
1 tablespoon mixed dried berries
1 tablespoon raisins
1 teaspoon slivered or sliced
almonds
1 teaspoon chopped walnuts

cooking instructions
In a bowl, mix the cereal with the yogurt. If too thick, add a little low-fat milk to thin out. Top with the mixed dried berries, raisins, almonds, and walnuts, and serve immediately.

Rye Bread with Cream Cheese and Salmon

✔ *Option: You may mix in a bit of freshly minced dill and some lemon juice into the cream cheese before spreading over the bread.*

serves 1

ingredients

1½ tablespoons low-fat cream cheese
1 slice rye bread
1 slice smoked salmon (about ¾ ounces)
Lemon juice

cooking instructions

Spread the cream cheese over the bread. Add the smoked salmon, sprinkle a little lemon juice, and serve immediately.

French Toast with Orange Slices

serves 4

✓ *For variety you may flavor with cinnamon and nutmeg.*

ingredients

3 eggs
⅔ cup low-fat milk
1½ teaspoons orange extract
8 slices whole wheat bread
4 tablespoons maple syrup
2 oranges, peeled and sliced
Pinch of salt
Vegetable oil

cooking instructions

Beat together the eggs, milk, orange extract, and salt. Dip the bread slices in the mixture. Soak them well.

Preheat two large skillets or a griddle with a little vegetable oil. Add the bread slices and brown on both sides. Serve immediately with maple syrup and orange slices.

Salmon and Asparagus Omelet

serves 4

ingredients

2 teaspoons canola oil
½ small onion, diced
1 garlic clove, minced
8 asparagus spears, cooked
1 teaspoon lemon juice
8 eggs
1 tablespoon low-fat milk
1 teaspoon minced fresh chives

1 teaspoon minced fresh dill
2 tablespoons minced fresh parsley
Salt and pepper to taste

cooking instructions

Heat the oil in a nonstick pan over medium heat. Add the onion and sauté until translucent. Add the garlic, asparagus and lemon juice, and sauté for 2 minutes. Spread the vegetables evenly on the bottom of the pan.

In a bowl, beat the eggs, milk, and herbs, and season with salt and pepper. Add the egg mixture to the vegetables in the pan and let the eggs set, about 1½ minutes. Add the smoked salmon, reduce heat, and continue to cook for 2 to 3 minutes. Fold the omelet over in half, cook for 1 more minute, and serve immediately.

Poached Eggs over Spinach

serves 4

ingredients

4 teaspoons olive oil (for the casseroles)
8 eggs
6 cups fresh baby spinach leaves
4 pinches nutmeg
4 pinches paprika
Salt and pepper to taste

cooking instructions

Grease 4 small casseroles with the oil and set aside. Fill a large pan with water and bring to a boil over high heat. Meanwhile, preheat a steamer. Place the spinach into the steamer basket and cook until the leaves are just barely wilted.

Reduce the heat under the boiling water to a gentle simmer. One by one, break the eggs into a cup and slide them into the simmering water. Throw away the shells. Make sure the eggs do not touch. Cook until the whites are set and firm to the touch (about 3 minutes).

Divide the spinach equally among the casseroles. Sprinkle nutmeg and season with salt and pepper. Using a slotted spoon, carefully remove each egg from the water, placing two each over the spinach in the casserole. Sprinkle with paprika and serve immediately.

Orange and Pumpkin Muffins

serves 12

ingredients

1½ cups gluten-free all-purpose baking flour
1½ teaspoons xanthan gum
½ cup flaxseed meal
⅓ cup honey
1 tablespoon baking powder
1 teaspoon baking soda
¼ teaspoon salt
1 teaspoon orange extract

1 teaspoon orange zest
2 tablespoons canola oil
2 large eggs
½ cup canned organic pumpkin puree
1 cup low-fat yogurt
12 tablespoons orange marmalade

✓ *You may substitute 2 eggs with 4 egg whites. Careful, this recipe can act like a laxative because pumpkin and flaxseed both have high diuretic properties. It is advisable to eat only one muffin per day.*

cooking instructions

Preheat the oven to 375°F. In a stand mixer, blend the flour, xanthan gum, flaxseed meal, honey, baking powder, baking soda, and salt. Blend in the orange extract, orange zest, canola oil, eggs, pumpkin puree, and yogurt, and mix until well incorporated.

Grease a 12-cup muffin pan. Fill each muffin cavity three quarters of the way up. Bake for 25 minutes or until cooked through with a golden brown crown.

Serve each muffin with 1 tablespoon of orange marmalade.

Breakfast Smoothie

serves 2

✔ *This breakfast smoothie also makes a perfect snack during the day.*

ingredients

4 ounces pure pomegranate juice, no sugar added
1 cup mixed berries
1 small banana
½ cup apple juice, no sugar added
1 tablespoon flaxseeds
Ice cubes

cooking instructions

Place all the ingredients in a blender and fill with ice. Puree on high speed until smooth. Divide between two tall glasses and serve immediately with a straw.

Strawberries, Pomegranate, and Spinach Smoothie

✔ *This breakfast smoothie can also be used for a snack during the day.*

serves 2

ingredients

2 cups strawberries
(about 10 ounces)
1 bunch fresh spinach
(at least 2 cups)
1 small banana

1 pomegranate
1 tablespoon flaxseeds
Ice cubes

cooking instructions

De-seed the pomegranate. Place the seeds in a blender and add the remaining ingredients. Fill with ice and puree on high speed until smooth. Divide between two tall glasses and serve immediately with a straw.

Soups & Salads

Pumpkin Soup

serves 6

> ✓ *The pumpkin seeds may be browned in the oven under the broiler for a stronger flavor.*

ingredients

One 3-pound pumpkin
1 teaspoon olive oil
2 large onions, sliced
(about 1 pound)
1 garlic clove, minced
6 cups chicken stock
(low-fat and low-sodium)
2 cups low-fat milk
2 fresh sage leaves

3 tablespoons low-fat Greek yogurt
2 tablespoons pumpkin seeds
Salt and pepper to taste

cooking instructions

Peel the pumpkin and cut the flesh into medium cubes.

Heat the oil in a large pan over high heat. Add the onions and sauté until translucent. Add the pumpkin, garlic, stock, milk, and sage, and bring to a boil. Reduce heat, cover, and simmer for 30 minutes. Transfer to a blender and puree with enough of the liquid to obtain a creamy consistency. Return to the pan, then season with salt and pepper. Before serving, add the yogurt and garnish with the pumpkin seeds.

Black Bean Soup

serves 6

✓ If the soup turns out too thick, adjust with stock. If the soup is too thin, reduce the liquid more.
Chicken stock may be substituted with vegetable stock.
Other beans may be substituted. Add spinach or chard for more greens.

ingredients

12 ounces dried black beans, rinsed
2 teaspoons canola oil
1 large onion, finely diced (about 8 ounces)
1 large carrot, finely diced (about 4 ounces)
2 large celery stalks, finely diced (about 4 ounces)

2 garlic cloves, minced
6 cups chicken stock (low-fat and low-sodium)
1 bouquet garni
Salt and pepper to taste

cooking instructions

Place the beans in a large pot and cover with water that comes up at least two inches above the beans' surface. Bring to a boil over high heat. Remove from heat and let soak for an hour. Drain and set aside.

Heat the oil in a large pan over high heat. Add the onion and sauté until translucent. Add the carrot, celery, and garlic, and cook for 2 minutes. Add the beans, stock, and bouquet garni, and bring to a boil. Reduce heat, cover, and simmer for 45 minutes or until the beans are cooked through. Skim the surface of any foam that forms as needed. Remove ⅓ cup of the bean and puree with a fork. Return to the bean soup and mix. Remove the bouquet garni, adjust seasonings and serve immediately.

Lentil Soup

serves 4

ingredients

2 teaspoons canola oil
1 large onion, finely diced
(about 8 ounces)
1 large carrot, finely diced
(about 4 ounces)
2 large celery stalks, finely diced
(about 4 ounces)
2 garlic cloves, minced
6 cups chicken stock
(low-fat and low-sodium)

✔ *If the soup turns out too thick, adjust with stock. If the soup is too thin, reduce the liquid after passing the ingredients through a sieve. Chicken stock may be substituted with vegetable stock. You may add 8 ounces of cooked ground turkey.*

1 small ham bone (optional)
3 cups lentils, rinsed
(about 12 ounces)
1 bouquet garni
Salt and pepper to taste

cooking instructions

Heat the oil in a large pan over high heat. Add the onion and sauté until translucent. Add the carrot, celery, and garlic, and cook for 2 minutes. Add the stock, ham bone (if using), lentils, and bouquet garni, and bring to a boil. Reduce heat, cover, and simmer for 35 minutes. Skim the surface to remove foam as needed. Continue to simmer uncovered for 10 minutes to thicken the soup. Remove any fat that may rise to the surface of the soup. Remove the ham bone and bouquet garni. Season with salt and pepper, and serve immediately.

Broccoli Soup

ingredients

2 teaspoons grapeseed oil
1 small onion, diced
(about 4 ounces)
4 large broccoli heads, chopped
(about 2 pounds)
1 garlic clove, minced
3 cups chicken or vegetable stock
(low-fat and low-sodium)

1 bouquet garni
1 cup low-fat milk
(cow's, soy, rice, or nut)
2 to 3 tablespoons cornstarch
mixed with a little water
Salt and pepper to taste

cooking instructions

Heat the oil in a large pan over high heat. Add the onion and sauté until translucent. Add three-quarters of the broccoli, the garlic, stock, and bouquet garni, and bring to a boil. Reduce heat and simmer until the broccoli is very tender. Remove the bouquet garni and puree with a hand blender. Add the milk and bring back to boil. Add the cornstarch mixture, a little at a time, until the desired consistency is obtained. Add the remaining broccoli and bring to a boil. Cook until the broccoli is tender, season with salt and pepper, and serve immediately.

Carrot and Apple Soup

serves 4

ingredients

5 large carrots, peeled and sliced (about 20 ounces)
1 large Golden Delicious apple, peeled and quartered (about 6 ounces)
1 medium onion, peeled and quartered (about 6 ounces)

4 cups chicken stock (low-fat and low-sodium)
1 bouquet garni
¼ teaspoon ground ginger
Salt and pepper to taste

cooking instructions

Place the carrots, apple, onion, stock, bouquet garni, and ginger in a large pan. Bring to boil over medium heat. Reduce heat, cover, and simmer until the vegetables are cooked through, 10 to 15 minutes. Transfer to a blender and puree with enough of the liquid to obtain a soup consistency. Season with salt and pepper and serve immediately.

Beet and Fennel Soup

✔ *Chicken stock may be substituted with vegetable stock.*

serves 4

ingredients

1 teaspoon canola oil
1 large onion, diced
(about 8 ounces)
1 small carrot, diced
(about 2 ounces)
1 large celery stalk, diced
(about 2 ounces)
1 garlic clove, minced
5 beets, peeled and chopped

3 fennel bulbs, cored, stems removed, and chopped
1 tablespoon minced fresh ginger
5 to 6 cups chicken stock
(low-fat and low-sodium)
2 tablespoons fresh orange juice
Salt and pepper to taste

cooking instructions

Heat the oil in a large pan over high heat. Add the onions and sauté until translucent. Add the carrot, celery, and garlic, and sauté for 2 minutes. Add the beets, fennel, ginger, stock, and orange juice, and bring to a boil. Reduce heat, cover, and simmer for 30 minutes. Transfer to a blender and puree with enough of the liquid to obtain the right consistency. Season with salt and pepper and serve immediately. You may also refrigerate for 2 hours before serving cold.

French Onion Soup

serves 4

ingredients

2 tablespoons grapeseed oil

3 large onions, thinly sliced (about 1½ pounds)

2 tablespoons Cognac (optional)

2 tablespoons flour

6 to 7 cups beef stock (low-fat and low-sodium)

¾ cup Swiss cheese or Gruyère, shredded (about 6 ounces)

Salt and pepper to taste

cooking instructions

Heat the oil in a large pan over medium heat. Add the onions and cook until golden brown. Stir occasionally to avoid burning. This will take up to 20 minutes. Carefully add the cognac and flambé (optional). Sprinkle with the flour and mix well. Add the beef stock and bring to a boil over high heat. Reduce heat and simmer for 20 to 25 minutes. Skim any foam or fat that may rise to the surface. Adjust seasonings and serve immediately with the cheese.

Squash Soup

serves 4

ingredients

2 large zucchini, peeled and sliced (about 12 ounces)

2 large yellow squash, peeled and quartered (about 12 ounces)

1 medium onion, peeled and quartered (about 6 ounces)

3½ cups chicken stock (low-fat and low-sodium)

1 bouquet garni

4 tablespoons freshly minced basil

4 tablespoons low-fat plain Greek yogurt

Salt and pepper to taste

cooking instructions

Place the zucchini, squash, onion, stock, and bouquet garni in a large pan. Bring to boil over medium heat. Reduce heat, cover, and simmer until the vegetables are cooked through, 10 to 15 minutes. Transfer to a blender and puree with enough of the liquid to obtain a soup consistency. Remove any remaining broth from the pan, return the pureed soup to it, add the basil, and season with salt and pepper. Bring to a boil and serve immediately. Top each serving with a tablespoon of yogurt.

Artichoke and Fava Bean Salad

serves 4

> ✓ *If fava beans are unavailable, use butter beans, broad beans, Windsor beans, or lima beans.*

ingredients

For the vinaigrette:
2 shallots, minced
1 large garlic clove, minced
1 teaspoon Dijon mustard
4 tablespoons balsamic vinegar
6 tablespoons olive oil
2 tablespoons flaxseed oil (or olive oil, if flaxseed oil unavailable)
3 tablespoons salad herbs
Salt and pepper to taste

For the salad:
4 ounces Boston lettuce
8 ounces cooked fava beans
1 cup cooked artichoke hearts
8 cherry tomatoes
4 ounces feta cheese, cut into 1-inch cubes
4 teaspoons slivered almonds

cooking instructions

For the vinaigrette: In a bowl, mix the shallots, garlic, mustard, and vinegar. Slowly whisk in the oils. Add the herbs and season with salt and pepper.

For the salad: Line a serving platter with the lettuce. Spread the fava beans, artichoke hearts, and tomatoes on top of the lettuce. Drizzle with the vinaigrette. Add the feta cheese and almonds, and serve immediately.

Chicken Salad with Celery and Apple

serves 4

ingredients

For the vinaigrette:
2 tablespoons cider vinegar
1 tablespoon lemon juice
2 teaspoons honey
2 tablespoons olive oil
1 tablespoon walnut oil
2 tablespoons fresh parsley, chopped
Salt and pepper to taste

For the salad:
2 large apples (about 12 ounces)
1 lemon, juiced
1 large heart of romaine, chopped (about 6 ounces)
12 ounces diced cooked chicken breast
2 large celery stalks, diced (about 4 ounces)
¼ cup walnuts, chopped

cooking instructions

For the vinaigrette: In a large bowl mix the vinegar, lemon juice, honey, oils, and parsley, and season with salt and pepper.

For the salad: Peel, core, and dice the apples. Mix them with some lemon juice to prevent browning. In a bowl, place the romaine, chicken, apples, and celery. Mix in the dressing, add the walnuts, and serve immediately.

Spinach, Strawberries, and Mango Salad

serves 4

ingredients

6 tablespoons pomegranate glaze (see recipe below)

4 tablespoons olive oil

1 teaspoon Dijon mustard

1 tablespoon freshly minced basil

4 cups baby spinach, washed and dried well

1 small red onion, thinly sliced

12 strawberries, washed, patted dry, and sliced

1 mango, peeled and sliced

2 ounces crumbled feta cheese

2 tablespoons chopped walnuts

Salt and pepper to taste

cooking instructions

In a bowl, mix 2 tablespoons pomegranate glaze, olive oil, Dijon mustard, and basil. Season with salt and pepper.

Place the baby spinach in a bowl and mix in the dressing. Divide among four plates. Top with red onion, strawberries, and mango. Sprinkle with feta cheese and walnuts. Drizzle the remaining 4 tablespoons of pomegranate glaze over and serve immediately.

To make pomegranate glaze: Bring 3 cups of organic pomegranate juice and 4 tablespoons of honey or agave nectar to a boil over medium heat. Reduce heat and simmer until reduced to ¾ cup. You can store the glaze in an airtight container for 2 weeks in the refrigerator.

Lentil Salad

serves 6

ingredients

For the dressing:
2 tablespoons wine vinegar
1 tablespoon minced shallot
1 teaspoon Dijon mustard
6 tablespoons walnut oil
3 tablespoons minced fresh salad
herbs
Salt and pepper to taste

For the salad:
1 pound lentils
1 tablespoon minced garlic
1 bouquet garni
1 bay leaf

cooking instructions

For the dressing: In a bowl, mix the vinegar, shallot, and mustard. Slowly whisk in the oil. Add the herbs, and season with salt and pepper.

For the salad: Rinse the lentils and place them in a pan. Add enough water to cover them completely. Bring to a boil over high heat. Remove from heat and set aside covered for 1 hour.

Drain and place in the large pan. Add water (3 times the volume of the lentils), the garlic, bouquet garni, and bay leaf, and bring to a boil over high heat. Reduce heat, cover, and simmer for 20 to 25 minutes or until tender.

Remove the bouquet garni and bay leaf. Drain the lentils and transfer to a bowl. Mix in the vinaigrette and refrigerate for 30 minutes. Serve cold.

Beets with Walnuts

serves 8

ingredients

For the salad:
2 large beets (about 20 ounces)
¼ cup walnuts, chopped

For the dressing:
1 small shallot, minced
1 large garlic clove, minced
1 teaspoon Dijon mustard

1½ tablespoons lemon juice
1 tablespoon minced fresh parsley
3 tablespoons walnut oil
Salt and pepper to taste

cooking instructions

For the salad: Place the beets in a large pan, cover with water, and bring to a boil over high heat. Reduce heat, cover, and simmer for 30 minutes or until cooked through. Drain and cool. Peel, slice, and place in a serving bowl.

For the dressing: In a bowl, mix the shallot, garlic, mustard, lemon juice, and parsley. Blend in the oil and season with salt and pepper.

Mix the beets with the dressing, sprinkle the walnuts over, and serve immediately.

Greens with Goat Cheese, Dates, and Walnuts

serves 4

ingredients

5 ounces mesclun
4 ounces goat cheese
¼ cup walnuts, chopped
8 Medjool dates
1 teaspoon Dijon mustard
1 large garlic clove, minced
1 large shallot, minced

2 tablespoons apple cider vinegar
2 tablespoons olive oil
2 tablespoons walnut oil
2 tablespoons salad herbs
Salt and pepper to taste

cooking instructions

In a bowl mix the mustard, garlic, shallot, and vinegar. Whisk in the oils, herbs, and season to taste.

Place the mesclun in a bowl and mix in ¾ of the vinaigrette. Crumble the goat cheese over the greens. Add the walnuts and dates. Drizzle the remaining dressing and serve immediately.

Belgium Endives with Gorgonzola

serves 4

ingredients

6 Belgium endives
(about 1 pound)
¼ cup walnuts, chopped
2 ounces Gorgonzola
2 tablespoons walnut oil
1 tablespoon red wine vinegar

1 tablespoon low-fat milk
mixed with a dash of mashed
Gorgonzola
1 tablespoon fresh salad herbs,
chopped
Salt and pepper to taste

cooking instructions

Mix the oil, vinegar, and milk mixture. Add herbs and season to taste.

Slice the endives. Discard the trunk of each endive. Wash and dry the
endives with a salad spinner. Transfer to a bowl and mix with the dressing.
Add the walnuts and the crumbled remaining Gorgonzola. Toss lightly
and serve immediately.

Carrot and Apple Salad

serves 4

ingredients

For the vinaigrette:
1 large garlic clove, minced
1 teaspoon Dijon mustard
2 tablespoons lemon juice
2 tablespoons canola oil
2 tablespoons flaxseed oil
(or canola oil, if flaxseed oil
unavailable)
1 tablespoon minced fresh parsley
Salt and pepper to taste

For the salad:
4 large carrots (about 1 pound)
1 large apple (about 6 ounces)
4 teaspoons walnuts

cooking instructions

For the vinaigrette: In a bowl, mix the garlic, mustard, and lemon juice. Blend in the oils. Add the parsley, and season with salt and pepper.

For the salad: Peel and shred the carrots, and immediately mix with the vinaigrette. Peel, core, and shred the apples, and immediately add to the carrots. Blend well and adjust seasonings. Add the walnuts and serve immediately.

Grapefruit and Crabmeat Salad

serves 2

ingredients

1 large pink grapefruit
(about 16 ounces)
8 ounces crabmeat portions,
excess water removed
2 tablespoons low-fat canola
mayonnaise

1 cup lettuce, shredded
1 tablespoon freshly minced
cilantro
Paprika to taste
Salt and pepper to taste

cooking instructions

Place the crabmeat in a bowl.

Cut the grapefruit in half. Insert a thin knife all around the skin to loosen up the flesh. Separate the flesh from the skin and place it on a cutting board. Dice the flesh small and transfer to the crabmeat bowl. Add mayonnaise, paprika, cilantro, and season to taste. Cover with plastic wrap and refrigerate for half an hour.

Equally divide the lettuce in two plates and top with the prepared grapefruit crabmeat salad.

Leeks with Walnut Vinaigrette

serves 4

ingredients

For the salad:
8 small leeks

For the vinaigrette:
1 large garlic clove, minced
1 large shallot, minced
¼ cup walnuts, finely chopped
1 teaspoon Dijon mustard

2 tablespoons tarragon vinegar
4 tablespoons walnut oil
2 tablespoons olive oil
1 tablespoon minced fresh chives
1 tablespoon minced fresh parsley
Salt and pepper to taste

cooking instructions

For the vinaigrette: In a bowl mix the garlic, shallot, walnuts, mustard, and vinegar. Slowly whisk in the oils. Add the chives and parsley, and season with salt and pepper.

For the leeks: Wash and trim the leeks. Place them in a pan, cover with water, and bring to a boil over high heat. Reduce heat, cover, and simmer for 10 minutes or until cooked through.

Drain and cut the leeks in half lengthwise. Mix the leeks with the vinaigrette and let cool. Refrigerate and serve cold.

Fish & Seafood Entrées

Salmon with Orange Sauce

serves 4

ingredients

For the fish:

2 oranges
1 teaspoon canola oil
Four 5-ounce salmon fillets
1 teaspoon coriander seeds, crushed
1 shallot, thinly sliced
1½ cups fresh orange juice
1 tablespoon honey

1 tablespoon cornstarch, mixed with a little water
1 teaspoon dried parsley
Salt and pepper to taste

For the vegetables:

2 pounds asparagus, trimmed (about 32 asparagus spears)
½ orange, juiced
Salt and pepper to taste

cooking instructions

Preheat the oven to 400°F.

For the fish: Zest the two oranges and julienne the zest. Blanch them for 2 minutes. Remove and set aside. Remove the white pith from the oranges and slice the oranges (into approximately ⅜-inch slices).

Grease the bottom of a baking pan with the oil. Add the salmon and season lightly with pepper. Cover the fillets with a pinch of crushed coriander, half of the zest, the shallot, and the oranges slices. Warm up ¼ cup of the juice with the remaining coriander. Pour the juice mixture over the fish, cover the baking pan with aluminum foil, and bake for 20 minutes or until the flesh start to flake. Transfer the fish and solids to a serving platter. Cover with aluminum foil to keep warm. Pour the remaining liquid from the baking pan into a saucepan. Add the remaining zest and juice and the honey. Bring to a boil and reduce to ¾ cup. Thicken with cornstarch mixture, a little at a time, until the desired consistency is obtained. Strain and return the liquid to the pan, discarding solids. Add the parsley and season with salt. Pour the sauce over the fish.

For the vegetables: Prepare a steamer. Add the asparagus and cook for 2 to 3 minutes or to desired taste. Transfer the asparagus to a serving plate, sprinkle a little orange juice, and season to taste.

Broiled Salmon with Dill

serves 4

✓ *This fish goes well with the Marinated Vegetables with Lemon.*

ingredients

Four 5-ounce salmon fillets
1 tablespoon olive oil
4 to 5 fresh dill branches, minced
Salt and pepper to taste

cooking instructions

Preheat the broiler. Rub some of the oil over the flesh side of the fillets. Lightly season with salt and pepper and spread the dill over. Place the fillets on a greased baking pan skin side up. Brush the remaining oil over the skin and broil for 3 to 4 minutes. Turn over and continue to broil for a few minutes or until the flesh starts to flake.

Salmon with Basil Aioli

serves 4

ingredients

For the aioli:
8 large garlic cloves
1 teaspoon salt
⅔ cup olive oil
2 tablespoons minced fresh basil
Pinch pepper

For the fish:
Four 5-ounce salmon fillets
2 teaspoons olive oil
Salt and pepper to taste

For the vegetables:
12 ounces baby carrots
Florets from 1 large head broccoli
(about 12 ounces)
1 lemon, quartered
Salt and pepper to taste

cooking instructions

Preheat the broiler.

For the aioli: All the ingredients must be at room temperature for the emulsion to take. In a food processor, puree the garlic and salt to a smooth paste. Pour in a drop of oil and mix until well incorporated. Continue the same way until most of the oil is incorporated. If you add the oil too quickly, the emulsion will not happen. Before adding the last drop of oil, blend in the basil and add a pinch of pepper.

For the fish: Place the salmon fillets on a greased baking pan. Brush 1 teaspoon of the oil over the fillets and season with salt and pepper. Broil 3 to 4 minutes. Turn over, brush with the remaining 1 teaspoon oil, season again, and continue to broil for 3 to 4 minutes more or until the flesh starts to flake.

For the vegetables: Preheat a steamer. Add the carrots and cook for 4 minutes. Add the broccoli and continue to cook for 2 minutes more. Transfer to a serving plate and season with salt and pepper.

Serve the salmon with the vegetables, aioli, and lemon wedges.

Honey Glazed Salmon

serves 4

ingredients

Four 5-ounce salmon fillets
2 tablespoons Dijon mustard
4 teaspoons honey
2 teaspoons freshly minced thyme
1 lime
Salt and pepper to taste

cooking instructions

Place the salmon fillets in a microwave safe dish.

In a bowl, mix the mustard, honey, thyme, and season to taste. Spread the mixture evenly over the salmon fillets. Sprinkle with a little lime juice and cover with a microwaveable top or loosely with plastic wrap. Microwave on high for 3 to 4 minutes. Time may vary based on the thickness of your fillets. Remove from the microwave and let stand for 2 minutes before serving.

Trout Greek Style

serves 4

ingredients

¼ teaspoon dried thyme

¼ teaspoon dried coriander

¼ teaspoon dried marjoram

¼ teaspoon dried rosemary

¼ teaspoon dried basil

Four 5-ounce whole trout

1 tablespoon olive oil

4 teaspoons minced fresh parsley

4 teaspoons minced fresh mint

1 lemon, juiced

Salt and pepper to taste

cooking instructions

Preheat the broiler.

For the fish: In a bowl blend the dried herbs. Place the trout on a flat surface and open their cavities. Sprinkle some salt, pepper, and a large pinch of the dried herbs in each trout. Add 1 teaspoon fresh parsley and 1 teaspoon fresh mint. Sprinkle lemon juice and close the trout. Place the trout on a greased baking pan. Drizzle the oil over the trout. Broil for 3 to 4 minutes. Carefully turn over, brush with oil, and continue to broil for another 3 to 4 minutes.

Trout with Horseradish

serves 4

ingredients

Four 5–ounce whole trout
1 tablespoon olive oil
3 tablespoons minced fresh parsley
4 tablespoons prepared horseradish sauce (store bought)
Salt and pepper to taste

cooking instructions

Preheat the broiler.

Clean the fish and pat dry. Sprinkle the inside of each trout with a little salt, pepper, oil, and parsley. Place the trout on a greased baking pan. Rub a little oil over the skin. Broil for 3 to 4 minutes. Carefully turn over, brush with oil, and continue to broil for another 3 to 4 minutes. Serve immediately with the prepared horseradish sauce.

Mackerel with Garlic Cloves

serves 4

ingredients

For the fish:
Four 5-ounce whole mackerel
16 garlic cloves, peeled
2 tablespoons olive oil
Salt and pepper to taste

For the vegetables:
4 large carrots, sliced
(about 1 pound)
3 large zucchini, sliced
(about 1 pound)
1 lemon, quartered
Salt and pepper to taste

cooking instructions

Preheat the oven to 400°F.

For the fish: Sprinkle a little salt and some pepper inside the mackerel cavities. Grease the bottom of a baking pan with a little of the oil. Blanch the garlic cloves in boiling water for 3 minutes. Slightly crush them on the bottom of the greased pan. Top them with the mackerel and drizzle the remaining oil over the fish. Bake for 20 to 25 minutes.

For the vegetables: Preheat a steamer. Add the carrots and cook for 4 minutes. Add the zucchini and continue to cook for 2 to 3 minutes or to desired doneness. Transfer to a serving platter and season to taste.

Serve the mackerel with the vegetables and lemon wedges.

Red Snapper en Papilotte

serves 4

ingredients

Four 5-ounce red snapper fillets
2 garlic cloves, minced
4 teaspoons freshly minced parsley
4 teaspoons capers
2 teaspoons lemon zest

4 teaspoons olive oil
4 tablespoons lemon juice
2 cups broccoli florets
2 cups sliced yellow squash
2 shallots, sliced
Pepper to taste

cooking instructions

Preheat the oven to 400°F.

Prepare four aluminum foil sheets. Place each fillet in the middle of one sheet and season lightly with pepper. Add the garlic, parsley, capers, shallot slices, and zest, dividing each equally among the sheets. Drizzle 1 teaspoon olive oil and 1 tablespoon lemon juice over each sheet. Fold the foil tightly closed. It must be completely sealed in order to form a papilotte. Place on a cookie sheet and bake for 10 to 15 minutes or until the fish starts to flake.

Meanwhile, prepare a steamer. Add the broccoli and yellow squash, and steam for 2 to 3 minutes or to desired tenderness. Serve immediately with the papilottes.

Tuna with Balsamic Vinegar

serves 4

ingredients

For the fish:
1 cup pearl onions
2 tablespoons olive oil
1½ cups balsamic vinegar
1 shallot, minced
1 large garlic clove, minced
1 tablespoon honey (optional)

Four 5-ounce tuna fillets
2 tablespoons minced fresh parsley
Salt and pepper to taste

cooking instructions

Preheat the broiler.

Blanch the onions in boiling water for 2 minutes. Drain, cool, and peel.

Heat 1 tablespoon of the oil in a skillet over medium heat. Add the onions and brown for two to three minutes. Add the vinegar, shallot, garlic, and honey (optional), then reduce by half.

Meanwhile, place the fillets on a greased baking pan. Brush a little of the remaining oil over the fish and lightly season with salt and pepper. Broil for 3 to 4 minutes. Turn over, drizzle the remaining oil, and continue to cook for a few minutes or until the flesh starts to flake.

Transfer the fish to a serving platter and top with the prepared onions.

Cod Fish with Leek Fondue

serves 4

ingredients

5 medium leeks
(about 1½ pounds)
1 tablespoon canola oil
¼ cup vegetable stock (low-fat
and low-sodium)
Four 5-ounce cod fillets
2 tablespoons crème fraiche
2 tablespoons lemon juice

1 tablespoon Dijon mustard
2 tablespoons freshly minced
chives
Salt and pepper to taste

For the vegetables:
3 medium potatoes, peeled and
quartered (about 1 pound)
3 large yellow squash, sliced in
1-inch pieces (about 1 pound)
Salt and pepper to taste

cooking instructions

Cut and discard the green part of the leeks. Cut the white part in half
and julienne. Wash well to remove any dirt and pat dry. Heat the oil in
a large sauté pan over high heat. Add the leeks and sauté for 2 minutes.
Add the stock and spread the leeks on the bottom of the pan. Place the
fish on top and sprinkle with pepper. Cover and cook for 20 minutes over
low heat. Meanwhile preheat the steamer. Add the potatoes and cook for
15 minutes. Add the squash and continue to cook for 5 minutes.

Remove the fish and set aside in a serving platter. Cover with
aluminum foil to keep warm. Add the lemon juice, mustard, crème
fraiche, and chives to the leeks. Mix well, adjust seasonings, and reduce
for 2 minutes. Pour the sauce over the fish and serve immediately with
the vegetables.

Baked Sardines with Collard Greens

serves 4

ingredients

Four 5-ounce sardines
2 tablespoons olive oil
1 large onion, sliced (about 8 ounces)
2 pounds collard greens; washed, ribs removed, and pat dry
3 garlic cloves, minced

⅓ cup low-fat milk
¼ cup fresh parsley, minced
1 teaspoon freshly minced thyme
2 pinches nutmeg
4 tablespoons shredded Parmesan
1 tablespoon almond meal
Salt and pepper to taste

cooking instructions

Preheat the oven to 375°F.

Remove the heads from sardines and clean their insides well (this can be done at the fish market). Rinse well under cold water.

Blanch the collard greens in salted water until barely tender. Drain and press to remove excess water. Chop the collard greens.

Heat 1 tablespoon olive oil in a nonstick pan over medium heat. Add the onion and sauté until translucent. Add the garlic, collard greens, and cook for 2 minutes mixing constantly. Sprinkle and mix in the almond meal. Add the milk, 2 tablespoons Parmesan, parsley, thyme, nutmeg, and season to taste.

Pour the mixture on to a greased baking dish and slide in the sardines. Sprinkle the remaining Parmesan and drizzle 1 tablespoon olive oil. Cover and bake for 20 to 25 minutes.

Poached Oysters with Leeks and Kale

serves 4

ingredients

1 tablespoon olive oil
24 oysters
1 shallot, minced
1 garlic clove, minced
2 large leeks (about 1 pound 6 ounces)
3 tablespoons crème fraiche

2 pounds kale
2 lemons
Salad herbs, minced
Pinch nutmeg
Salt and pepper to taste

cooking instructions

Trim the leeks keeping only the white part. Cut in half, clean, and chop small.

Carefully open the oysters and transfer their water to a bowl. Remove their flesh and set aside. Place the shells in a large bowl. Zest half a lemon.

Blanch the kale in salted water until tender. Press to remove excess water. Chop small and set aside.

Heat a large pan with water and bring to boil. Meanwhile heat the oil in a pan over high heat. Add the shallot, garlic, leek, and sauté until tender. Add the kale, a little lemon juice, lemon zest, nutmeg, oyster water, herbs, and crème fraiche. Stir well and bring to a simmer. Reduce heat and add the oysters. Season to taste and continue to cook another minute. Blanch the oyster shells in the boiling water and transfer to a serving platter. Fill each oyster shell with the prepared mixture and serve immediately with lemon wedges.

Sablefish with Honey and Thyme

serves 4

ingredients

¼ cup honey
¼ cup white Muscat
1 cup vegetable stock
(low-sodium)
1 teaspoon minced fresh thyme

Four 5-ounce sablefish fillets
1 tablespoon olive oil
1 tablespoon lemon juice
2 tablespoons minced fresh
parsley
Salt and pepper to taste

cooking instructions

Combine the honey, wine, stock, and thyme in a saucepan. Bring to a boil over high heat. Reduce heat and reduce to ¾ cup.

Heat the oil in a nonstick pan over medium heat. Lightly season the fillets with salt and pepper, add the fillets to the pan, and brown for two to three minutes. Turn over carefully and cook for 1 minute more. Add the lemon juice and continue to cook for 2 to 3 minutes. Pour in the prepared sauce and parsley, and bring to a boil. Adjust the seasonings and serve immediately.

Scallops with Tangerines

serves 4

ingredients

6 tangerines
1 cup orange juice
1 teaspoon minced ginger
3 teaspoons olive oil, plus more
for drizzling
1 pound scallops

1 shallot, minced
8 ounces mushrooms
2 tablespoons minced fresh
parsley
Salt and pepper to taste

cooking instructions

Peel and segment the tangerines. Place the orange juice and half of the
ginger in a saucepan and bring to a boil over high heat. Reduce to ¼
cup and set aside.

Heat 1 teaspoon oil in a saucepan over high heat. Add the mushrooms,
shallot, and remaining ginger, and sauté briefly. Add parsley and lightly
season with salt and pepper. Heat the remaining 2 teaspoons oil in a
large saucepan over high heat. Lightly season the scallops, add to the
pan, and sear for 1½ minutes. Turn over and sear for 1½ minutes more.
Add the tangerine segments, reduced orange juice, and continue to
sauté for 1 minute. Serve immediately with the mushrooms and drizzle
a little oil.

Meat, Poultry & Vegetarian Entrées

Roasted Chicken Breast with Garlic Cloves

serves 4

✓ *Serve with Steamed Vegetables (see page 91) and lemon wedges.*

ingredients

Four 6-ounces chicken breasts
with bones and skin
8 to 10 garlic cloves
4 teaspoons olive oil
1 tablespoon dried Italian herbs
1 large lemon, cut in 8 slices

2 pinches of coarse salt
Pepper to taste

cooking instructions

Preheat the oven to 375°F. Mince the garlic cloves on a clean cutting board. Sprinkle the coarse salt over the minced garlic cloves. Press with the side of a chef's knife until you end up with smooth paste. Transfer to a bowl. Mix in the olive oil, Italian herbs, and season with pepper. With your fingers, carefully separate the chicken skin slightly from the flesh, being careful not to break the skin. Spread the garlic mixture over the chicken flesh, add 2 lemon slices per breast, and push back the skin. Place the breasts in a baking dish and bake for 20 to 25 minutes, or until cooked through. Time may vary depending on the thickness of the breasts. Serve immediately and discard skin when eating.

Chicken Breast with Asian Glaze

serves 4

ingredients

Four 5-ounce chicken breasts
with bones and skin
2 tablespoons maple syrup
1 tablespoon green tea leaves
1 tablespoon Oriental
hot mustard

1 garlic clove, minced
2 tablespoons sesame seeds
1 teaspoon ground ginger
Canola oil
Salt and pepper to taste

cooking instructions

Preheat the oven to 350°F. Wash and pat dry the chicken breasts. Carefully pass your fingers between the meat and the skin to loosen up the skin without breaking it.

Heat the maple syrup, tea, mustard, garlic, and ginger in a saucepan over low heat until well blended. Season to taste and set aside. Lift up the chicken skin and brush the mixture over the chicken meat. Sprinkle the sesame seeds under the skin. Brush canola oil over the skin and roast for 30 minutes, or until cooked through. Remove skin before serving.

Chicken Breast with Dijon Mustard

✓ *Serve with Steamed Vegetables (see page 155)*

serves 4

ingredients

Four 5-ounce skinless chicken breasts
1 tablespoon Dijon mustard
2 teaspoons lemon juice
½ teaspoon garlic powder
Canola oil
Salt and pepper to taste

cooking instructions

Preheat the oven to 375°F. Place the chicken breasts in a lightly oiled pan. In a bowl, mix the mustard, lemon juice, and garlic powder. Spread over the chicken breasts and season to taste. Bake for 20 to 25 minutes, or until cooked through. Time may vary depending on the thickness of the breasts.

Stuffed Chicken Breast with Boursin

serves 4

ingredients

Four 4-ounce chicken breasts

4 pinches dried Italian herbs

2 ounces Boursin (garlic and herbs), divided into four portions

8 fresh large basil leaves

1 tablespoon olive oil, plus more for stir-frying

1 large shallot, thinly sliced

1 cup chicken stock (low-fat and low-sodium)

Cornstarch mixed with a little water

2 tablespoons minced fresh parsley

2 pounds fresh dandelions, washed and pat dry

Kitchen twine or toothpicks

Salt and pepper to taste

cooking instructions

Preheat the oven to 350°F. Place the chicken breasts between two plastic wrap sheets. Flatten with a mallet until fairly thin. Sprinkle pepper and a pinch of Italian herbs on each breast. Spread one portion of Boursin and 2 basil leaves, and roll each breast tightly. Secure with kitchen twine so they do not unroll. Heat the oil in an ovenproof sauté pan over high heat. Add the turkey rolls, side face down, and brown for two to three minutes. Turn over and brown two minutes more. Once browned, add the shallot and ½ cup of the chicken stock. Bring to a boil and place in the oven for 10 to 12 minutes. Remove the rolls from the pan and place on a serving platter. Cover with aluminum foil to keep warm. Add the remaining ½ cup stock to the pan (be careful, it just came out of the oven) and reduce the sauce to a little less than 1 cup. Thicken with a little cornstarch mixture. Add the parsley and any rendered turkey juices, and bring to a boil. Adjust seasonings and pour over the turkey. Serve immediately with the steamed dandelions. While the sauce is reducing, stir-fry the dandelions until slightly wilted. Season to taste and serve with the stuffed chicken.

Lemon Chicken

serves 4

✓ *This lemon chicken can also be used for appetizers, salads, soups, etc.*

ingredients

3 tablespoons olive oil
5 lemons, 4 juiced, 1 cut into wedges
1 tablespoon freshly minced poultry herbs
Four 4-ounce skinless chicken breasts
Pepper to taste

cooking instructions

Mix in 2 tablespoons of the oil, the juice, and herbs, and season with pepper. Place the chicken pieces in a plastic bag. Pour the lemon marinade over the chicken and refrigerate for at least one hour rotating every 10 minutes.

Preheat the broiler. Remove the chicken breasts from the marinade and pat dry. Place them on a cookie sheet greased with a little of the remaining 1 tablespoon oil and brush the rest of the remaining oil over each breast. Broil for approximately 6 to 7 minutes on each side. Watch carefully to avoid burning. Serve immediately with the lemon wedges.

Roasted Chicken Au Jus

serves 4 to 6

ingredients

1 whole chicken (4 pounds)

2 teaspoons dried thyme, minced

2 teaspoons dried rosemary, minced

1 small onion, cut into 4 pieces (about 4 ounces)

1 medium carrot, cut into 4 pieces (about 3 ounces)

1 celery stalk, cut into 2 pieces

2 cups chicken stock (low-fat and low-sodium)

Canola oil

1 tablespoon cornstarch, mixed with a little water

Salt and pepper to taste

cooking instructions

Preheat the oven to 325°F.

Remove giblets from the chicken. Rinse chicken and pat dry. Season the chicken cavity and add 1 teaspoon each of the thyme and rosemary. Brush some oil over the chicken. Sprinkle the remaining 1 teaspoon each herbs and season with salt and pepper. Place the chicken in a roasting pan and roast for 2 to 2½ hours or until the juices run clear. Remove the chicken from the pan and set aside covered to keep warm. Remove excess fat from the roasting pan. Add the onion, carrot, celery, and chicken stock, and deglaze pan. Bring to boil over medium heat and reduce to 1 cup. Strain, discard solids, place the liquid in a saucepan, add any rendered chicken juices, and bring to boil. Thicken with cornstarch mixture, a little at a time, until the desired consistency is obtained. Serve immediately with the chicken.

Chicken Burgers with Lettuce Wraps

serves 4

ingredients

2 white anchovy fillets

4 tablespoons garlic Caesar Litehouse Foods dressing

Four 4-ounce organic chicken burgers

2 tablespoons olive oil

4 garlic cloves, minced

16 lettuce leaves

4 tablespoons Parmesan cheese

Canola oil

Salt and pepper to taste

cooking instructions

In a food processor, puree the anchovy fillets with the dressing. Add a little water to thin out. Lightly season the burgers with salt and pepper and shape them to fit in the lettuce leaves. Do not allow the meat to touch the leaves. Heat up the olive oil with the garlic. Remove at first boil and set aside.

Preheat the grill to medium-high heat. Grease the grill with canola oil before adding the burgers. Cook them for 3 to 5 minutes on each side or until cooked through. Meanwhile, carefully brush the garlic oil over the lettuce leaves.

Place two leaves on a plate, top with one burger, spread 1 tablespoon of the dressing, sprinkle 1 tablespoon cheese, and fold any lettuce overhang over the top. Top with 2 more leaves and tuck underneath to seal. Repeat with the remaining ingredients. Serve immediately with your favorite sides. Use toothpick to hold the lettuce in place if necessary.

Turkey Breast with Italian Herbs

serves 8

ingredients

4 teaspoons dried Italian herbs
One 2-pound skin-on turkey breast
1 tablespoon olive oil
1 bunch fresh basil leaves
¼ cup chicken stock (low-fat and low-sodium)*
Pepper to taste

You may need an extra ¼ cup or more of chicken stock to keep the chicken moist throughout the cooking process.

cooking instructions

Preheat the oven to 350°F.

Mix 3 teaspoons of the herbs with a little pepper. Carefully pass your fingers between the meat and the skin to loosen up the skin without breaking it. Spread the herb mixture on the flesh. Add as many basil leaves as you can fit under the skin without breaking it. Brush the oil over the skin.

Place the turkey breast skin side up in a roasting pan. Pour the stock into the pan, add the remaining 1 teaspoon herbs, and bake for 1 hour or until a meat thermometer inserted into the thickest part of the breast registers 180°F. Keep moistening with chicken stock. Do not allow the pan to get dry in order to keep the turkey breast moist. Transfer the turkey breast to a platter and let cool before slicing.

Stuffed Turkey Breast Italian Style

serves 4

ingredients

Four 4-ounce skinless turkey breasts

4 pinches dried Italian herbs

4 slices prosciutto ham

2 ounces goat cheese, sliced in 4 pieces

8 large fresh basil leaves

1 tablespoon olive oil

1 large shallot, thinly sliced

¼ cup Madeira

1 cup chicken stock (low-fat and low-sodium)

Cornstarch mixed with a little water

2 tablespoons minced fresh parsley

Toothpicks or kitchen twine

Salt and pepper to taste

cooking instructions

Preheat the oven to 350°F.

Place the turkey breasts between two plastic wrap sheets. Flatten with a mallet until fairly thin. Lightly season with salt and pepper, and sprinkle a pinch of Italian herbs on each breast. To each breast add one slice of ham, one slice of cheese, and 2 basil leaves, and roll tightly. Secure with a few toothpicks so they do not unroll.

Heat the oil in an ovenproof sauté pan over high heat. Add the turkey rolls, folded side down, and brown, about two to three minutes. Turn over and sauté, two minutes more. Once browned, add the shallot, Madeira, ½ cup of the chicken stock. Bring to a boil and place in the oven for 10 to 12 minutes. Remove the rolls from the oven and place on a serving platter. Cover with aluminum foil to keep warm. Add the remaining ½ cup stock to the pan (be careful, it just came out of the oven!) and reduce the sauce to with a little less than 1 cup. Thicken with a little cornstarch mixture. Add the parsley and any rendered turkey juices, and bring to a boil. Adjust seasonings and pour over the turkey.

Duck Breast with Berries

serves 6

ingredients

½ cup wild rice
Four 6-ounce duck breasts
1 teaspoon grapeseed oil
1 shallot, sliced ·
2 tablespoons red wine vinegar
½ cup Zinfandel or Syrah
1 cup chicken stock (low-fat and low-sodium)

8 ounces blueberries
1 fresh thyme branch
1 fresh rosemary sprig
2 juniper berries
Cornstarch mixed with a little water
Salt and pepper to taste

cooking instructions

Cook the rice according to package instructions. Heat the oil in an ovenproof sauté pan over high heat. Lightly season the underside of the duck breasts with salt and pepper, add to the pan skin side down, and sauté until golden brown, approximately 3 minutes. Turn over and cook for 2 minutes more. Place in the oven for 5 minutes (rare) to 10 minutes (well-done). Remove the breasts from the pan and place on a serving platter. Cover with aluminum foil to keep warm.

Discard excess fat from the pan. Add the shallot, vinegar, and wine, then boil until reduced by half. Add the stock, half of the blueberries, thyme, rosemary, and juniper berries, then boil until reduced by half. Pass through a sieve, pressing hard to extract all the juices, and return the liquid to the pan. Add any juices rendered by the duck breasts and bring to a boil. Reduce a little more and thicken with a little cornstarch mixture. Adjust seasonings and add the remaining blueberries. Bring to a boil and pour over the duck breasts. Serve immediately with the wild rice.

Pork Loins with Prunes

serves 4

ingredients

1 tablespoon grapeseed oil
Four 5-ounce pork loins,
seasoned lightly with pepper
1 medium onion, quartered
(about 6 ounces)
1 large carrot, quartered
(about 4 ounces)
½ cup seedless white grapes
1½ pounds prunes, pitted

½ cup white grape juice,
unsweetened
1 cup beef stock
(low-fat and low-sodium)
1 bay leaf
½ teaspoon thyme
Salt and pepper to taste

cooking instructions

Heat 2 teaspoons oil in a saucepan over high heat. Add the onion and
slightly brown. Add the carrot and sauté for 2 minutes. Add the prunes,
grapes, grape juice, beef stock, and bring to a boil. Reduce heat, cover,
and simmer for 20 to 25 minutes. Adjust seasoning.

Heat one teaspoon of oil in a saucepan over high heat. Add the fillets
and brown on both sides. Reduce heat and continue to cook for 3 to 4
minutes or until cooked through. Deglaze the pan with a little bit of the
prune juices and adjust seasoning. Serve immediately with the remaining
prunes mixture.

Tofu and Collard Greens Burgers

serves 4

ingredients

8 ounces tofu
6 ounces cooked collard greens
1 small onion, diced
(about 4 ounces)
1 small carrot, shredded
(about 2 ounces)
2 scallions, chopped
2 garlic cloves, minced
1⅓ cups water crackers

4 teaspoons almond butter
2 tablespoons minced salad herbs
4 slices cheddar cheese (about 4
ounces)
Salt and pepper to taste

cooking instructions

Mix all the ingredients, except cheese, in a food processor until well combined. Form 4 patties and grill on each side for 4 to 5 minutes. Melt the cheese on top and serve immediately.

Side Dishes & Snacks

Wild Rice with Vegetables

serves 8

ingredients

1⅓ cups wild rice
2 teaspoons olive oil
2 medium onions, finely diced
(about 12 ounces)
2 medium carrots, finely diced
(about 6 ounces)
3 large celery stalks, finely diced
(about 6 ounces)

1 garlic clove, minced
4 cups vegetable stock
2 tablespoons minced fresh parsley
1 teaspoon minced fresh ginger
Salt and pepper to taste

cooking instructions

Rinse the rice well and drain. Heat the oil in a deep pan over high heat. Add the onions, carrots, celery, and garlic, then sauté for 2 minutes. Add the rice and sauté for 1 minute. Add the stock, parsley, and ginger then bring to a boil. Cover, reduce heat, and cook until tender (approximately 45 minutes but it may depend of the type of rice you use. For best results, see package instructions). Season with salt and pepper and remove from heat. If necessary, strain and serve immediately.

Rice with Lentils

serves 8

ingredients

2½ cups lentils, rinsed
2 teaspoons olive oil
2 large onions, diced
(about 1 pound)
2 teaspoons minced garlic
1 teaspoon ground cumin
1 teaspoon ground coriander

1 teaspoon paprika
2 tablespoons minced fresh
parsley
1⅓ cups long-grain rice, rinsed
Salt and pepper to taste

cooking instructions

Place the lentils in a pan and add enough water to cover them. Bring to a boil over high heat and simmer for 10 minutes. Drain and set aside.

Heat the oil in a large pan over high heat. Add the onions and sauté until translucent. Add the garlic, lentils, cumin, coriander, paprika, and parsley, and season with salt and pepper. Add 6 cups water. Bring to a boil, reduce heat, cover, and simmer for 10 minutes. Add the rice and bring to a boil. Reduce heat, cover, and cook for 20 minutes or until tender. Adjust seasonings and remove from heat. Set aside covered for 5 minutes before serving.

Brown Rice Pilaf

serves 4

ingredients

½ cup brown rice
1 teaspoon olive oil
1 medium onion, finely diced
(about 6 ounces)
1 medium carrot, finely diced
(about 3 ounces)
¼ cup fresh corn
¼ cup fresh peas

1 small garlic clove, minced
1 cup vegetable stock
1 tablespoon minced fresh parsley
Salt and pepper to taste

cooking instructions

Rinse the rice twice and drain. Heat the oil in a deep pan over high heat. Add the onion, carrot, corn, peas, and garlic, and sauté for 2 minutes. Add the rice and sauté for a minute. Add the stock and parsley, and bring to a boil. Cover, reduce heat, and cook until tender (approximately 40 minutes but it may depend of the type of rice you use. For best results, see package instructions). Season with salt and pepper and remove from heat. If necessary, drain and serve immediately.

Steamed Vegetables

serves 4

ingredients

1 lemon, juiced

2 tablespoons minced fresh salad herbs

2 cups baby carrots (about 8 ounces)

½ small head cauliflower, chopped (about 8 ounces)

Florets from 1 medium head broccoli (about 8 ounces)

Salt and pepper to taste

cooking instructions

Steaming is a very fast cooking process, so pay attention because your vegetables can overcook very quickly. Cut the vegetables the same size for even cooking.

Mix the lemon juice and 1 tablespoon of the salad herbs, and season with salt and pepper. Set aside.

Preheat a steamer. When the water is boiling, add the carrots and cauliflower florets in even layers to ensure uniform cooking. Cook covered for 4 minutes. Add the broccoli florets, cover, and cook for 1 to 2 minutes more. Transfer the vegetables to a serving bowl and mix in the lemon juice mixture.

Top with the remaining 2 tablespoons salad herbs and serve immediately.

Marinated Vegetables with Lemon

serves 4

ingredients

For the marinade:
1 lemon
1 tablespoon minced garlic
1 branch fresh thyme, minced
1 teaspoon honey
1 tablespoon rice vinegar
3 tablespoons olive oil
1 teaspoon dried parsley
Salt and pepper to taste

For the vegetables:
1 large onion (about 8 ounces)
2 large carrots (about 8 ounces)
8 asparagus spears
(about 8 ounces)
Florets from 1 medium head
broccoli (about 8 ounces)

cooking instructions

For the marinade: Remove zest from the lemon, mince, and place in a bowl. Juice the lemon and add to the bowl. Blend in the remaining marinade ingredients and set aside.

For the vegetables: Cut the vegetables the same size for even cooking. Parboil the carrots for 2 minutes and place immediately in ice-cold water to stop the cooking process. Drain and set aside.

Place all the vegetables in a plastic bag, add the marinade, mix well, and refrigerate for at least 4 hours.

Preheat the oven to 450°F. Transfer the vegetables and marinade to a baking pan. Bake for 20 to 25 minutes or to desired tenderness.

Green Beans with Mushrooms

serves 4

ingredients

1 pound green beans, ends trimmed
1½ tablespoons olive oil
1 small onion, sliced (about 4 ounces)
½ cup mushrooms, sliced
2 garlic cloves, minced

2 pinches minced fresh thyme
2 tablespoons minced fresh basil
1 tablespoon minced fresh parsley
Salt and pepper to taste

cooking instructions

Place the greens beans in a large pan and fill with enough water to cover them. Add 1 teaspoon of salt and bring to a boil over high heat. Reduce heat and simmer until cooked through. Drain and set aside.

Heat 1 tablespoon of oil in a nonstick pan over medium heat. Add the onion and sauté until translucent. Add the garlic, mushrooms, and herbs, and sauté for 2 minutes. Blend in the green beans, and remaining oil. Season with salt and pepper, and serve immediately.

Asparagus au Gratin

serves 4

ingredients

1½ pounds asparagus (about 24 asparagus)
2 ounces shredded Parmesan cheese (about ¾ cup)
¼ cup Italian breadcrumbs
2 tablespoons grapeseed oil
½ teaspoon dry mustard
1 tablespoon dried parsley
Salt and pepper to taste

cooking instructions

Preheat the oven to 400°F and a steamer.

Trim the asparagus and add them to the steamer basket..Cook for 2 minutes covered. Transfer the asparagus to a greased baking sheet. In a bowl, mix together the cheese, breadcrumbs, oil, mustard, parsley, and season to taste. Spread over the asparagus and bake for 10 minutes or until the mixture is golden brown.

Vegetables with Tapenade

serves 4

ingredients

3 ounces black olives, pitted
4 anchovy fillets, rinsed
and pat dry
3 teaspoons capers
1 small garlic clove
2 tablespoons olive oil

Vegetables such as carrots,
cucumbers, cauliflower florets,
and mushrooms
Lemon juice to taste
Pepper to taste

cooking instructions

In a food processor puree the olives, anchovies, capers, and garlic. Add pepper to taste. Slowly add the olive oil until you obtain a smooth paste. Add lemon juice to taste. Serve with mixed vegetables.

Roasted Pumpkin

serves 4

ingredients

3 pounds sugar pumpkin
1 tablespoon grapeseed oil
Pumpkin pie spices mix
Salt and pepper to taste

✔ *You can also use the cooked pumpkin to make a puree or soup. Thin out with low-fat milk until the necessary consistency is reached. You can also use the cooked pumpkin as a base for dips or as a dessert base.*

cooking instructions

Cut open the pumpkin, remove seeds and clean the inside with a spoon. Brush oil inside the cavity, season to taste, and place opening side down on a baking sheet. Roast for 30 to 45 minutes or until tender. Cut out and sprinkle with a little pumpkin pie spices before serving.

Broccoli and Pistachio Vinaigrette

serves 4

ingredients

1 teaspoon Dijon mustard
1 tablespoon minced shallots
1 teaspoon minced garlic
4 tablespoons olive oil
3 tablespoons lemon juice
1 tablespoon minced fresh parsley

Florets from 2½ large heads broccoli (about 1½ pounds)
4 teaspoons chopped pistachios
Salt and pepper to taste

cooking instructions

In a bowl, mix the mustard, shallot, garlic, oil, lemon juice, and parsley, and season with salt and pepper.

Preheat a steamer. Add the broccoli and cook for 2 to 3 minutes or to desired doneness. Heat the vinaigrette in a pan over medium heat until warm. Transfer the cooked broccoli to a bowl. Pour the warmed vinaigrette and toss. Sprinkle the pistachios and serve immediately.

Carrots with Mashed Avocado

serves 2

✓ *Option: add a few drops of Tabasco® for a spicy touch*

ingredients

½ avocado
½ lemon, juiced
20 baby carrots

cooking instructions

Mash the avocado and mix in the lemon juice. Serve immediately with the carrots.

Yogurt with Flaxseeds

serves 1

ingredients

½ cup low-fat plain yogurt
1 tablespoon ground flaxseeds

✔ *For added flavor, try using fresh fruits/ berries, preserves, compotes, nuts/seeds or vegetables such as cucumber or pureed avocado with a drizzle of olive oil or walnut oil.*

cooking instructions

Mix the yogurt with the flaxseeds and serve immediately.

Spinach with Pine Nuts and Raisins

serves 4

ingredients

2 tablespoons grapeseed oil
⅓ cup plump raisins
1 tablespoon pine nuts
2 pounds fresh spinach, washed and patted dry
Salt and pepper to taste

cooking instructions

Heat the oil in a nonstick pan over medium heat. Add the raisins, pine nuts, and sauté for 1 minute. Add the spinach and sauté very briefly. Season with salt and peper and serve immediately. The spinach should be barely wilted to avoid turning to mush.

Apple and Walnut Bruschetta

24 bruschetta

ingredients

1 fresh rosemary sprig
1 lemon, juiced
6 apples, washed and patted dry
(about 2¼ pounds)
1 tablespoon canola oil
1 walnut bread loaf
Two 5-ounce goat cheese logs,
thinly sliced

6 tablespoons honey
½ cup walnuts, finely chopped
Salt and pepper to taste

cooking instructions

Mince the rosemary as small as possible. Mix with some of the the
lemon juice. Peel, core, and quarter the apples. Slice each quarter into 3
slices. Place the apples in a bowl, mix in the rosemary-flavored lemon
juice, and set aside.

Pat the apples slices dry with paper towels. Heat the oil in a large sauté
pan over high heat. Add the slices and brown them slightly. Remove
the apples and set aside. The apples must still be slightly crunchy. Add a
little water and the remaining lemon juice to deglaze the pan. Swirl and
scrape to dissolve cooked particles on the bottom and side of the pan.
Reduce to approximately 1 tablespoon. Strain over the apples and mix
carefully.

Preheat the broiler. With a serrated knife, cut the bread into ¾-inch-
thick slices. Cut each slice in half. Place the slices on a baking sheet.
Broil on both sides until golden brown. Cool before use.

Add 3 apple slices to each toasted bread slice. Lay a thin slice of goat
cheese and season with salt and pepper. Place under the broiler and
melt the cheese slightly. Pour ¼ teaspoon of honey over each slice and
sprinkle with walnuts. Serve immediately.

Salmon Bruschetta

24 bruschetta

ingredients

1⅓ cup fresh basil
⅔ cup fresh parsley
2 tablespoons minced
fresh lemon thyme
½ cup walnuts
2 garlic cloves
1 lemon, zested and juiced
¼ cup olive oil

1 country bread loaf
24 smoked salmon slices, rolled
(about 1 pound 2 ounces)
Salt and pepper to taste

cooking instructions

In a food processor, puree the basil, parsley, lemon thyme, walnuts, garlic, 1 tablespoon lemon zest, and 1 tablespoon lemon juice. Gradually add the oil until you have a smooth paste. Season with salt and pepper. If too thick, add a little more oil.

Preheat the broiler. With a serrated knife, cut the walnut bread into ½-inch-thick slices. Cut each slice in half. Place the slices on a baking sheet. Broil on both sides until golden brown. Cool before using.

Spread some paste over each bread slice. Add one salmon roll, sprinkle each with a little lemon juice, and serve immediately.

Desserts

Cottage Cheese with Fruit

serves 4

ingredients

½ cup low-fat cottage cheese, chilled
¼ cup blackberries
1 tablespoon dried apricots
1 tablespoon raisins
1 teaspoon ground flaxseeds

cooking instructions

Mix the cottage cheese with the flaxseeds. Add the blackberries, dry fruits, and serve immediately.

Fruit Salad with Mint

serves 4

> ✓ As an alternative, you can try substituting white or green tea leaves for the mint leaves in this recipe.

ingredients

1 tablespoon lemon juice
1 mint tea sachet
1 tablespoon honey
1 small banana, sliced
3 ounces strawberries, halved
3 ounces blueberries

3 ounces raspberries
1 small apple, cubed
2 large plums, pitted and quartered
2 tablespoons chopped fresh mint leaves
¼ cup pomegranate seeds

cooking instructions

Boil ¾ cup water. Add the lemon juice, tea sachet, and honey, then infuse to desired strength. Remove sachet and cool completely.

Mix all the fruits in a large bowl. Add the cold tea and refrigerate for 30 minutes, mixing every 10 minutes. Mix in the fresh mint and pomegranate seeds, then serve immediately.

Yogurt with Prunes

serves 4

ingredients

1 pound prunes
3 ounces sugar
12 ounces water
16 ounces low-fat Greek yogurt

cooking instructions

Soak the prunes in water for two hours. Transfer to a pan, add the sugar, and bring to a simmer over medium heat. Reduce heat and continue to cook for 1 hour. Remove from heat and let cool. Refrigerate until cold.

Divide the yogurt into four serving bowls, top with the prunes, and serve immediately.

Apple with Almond Butter

serves 1

ingredients

1 apple
1 tablespoon almond butter

cooking instructions

Cut out four pieces of apple around its core. Spread with the almond butter and serve immediately.

Peach with Apricot Coulis

serves 8

ingredients

4 peaches
12 apricots
1 tablespoon honey
1 teaspoon lemon juice
1 rosemary branch
4 teaspoons almonds

cooking instructions

Cut apricots in half and remove pits. Place the apricots in a pan. Add
½ cup water, honey, rosemary, lemon juice, and bring to a boil. Reduce
heat, cover, and simmer for ten minutes. Puree in a blender and transfer
to a serving bowl. Let cool and refrigerate. Peel and cut the peaches
in half. Place the peach halves on a serving platter, drizzle with some
apricot sauce and the almonds. Serve with the remaining apricot sauce
on the side.

Red Fruit Compote

serves 4

✔ *Suggestion: Serve with low-fat yogurt, sherbet, cream of millet, apple slices, etc.*

ingredients

8 ounces blackberries

8 ounces raspberries

8 ounces blueberries

8 ounces strawberries

3 tablespoons honey

1 large organic lemon peel

1 large organic orange peel

1 cup pomegranate juice (no sugar added)

Cornstarch mixed with a little water

cooking instructions

Wash the berries and carefully pat dry. Place the pomegranate juice in a saucepan and bring to boil over high heat. Reduce by half. If necessary, thicken with a little water-cornstarch mixture. Add the honey, berries, and cook for a minute or two. Do not overcook, or you will end up with a sauce rather than a compote. Remove from heat and transfer the compote to a bowl. Place the bowl in an ice-cold water bath to stop the cooking process. Refrigerate for two hours before serving.

Baked Apples with Cranberries

serves 4
1 serving: 1 apple

ingredients

4 large apples
3 tablespoons red currant jelly
4 tablespoons cranberry juice
4 teaspoons walnuts
4 teaspoons cranberries

cooking instructions

Preheat the oven to 400°F.

Wash and core the apples, being careful not to break through the bottom of the apples. Place them in a baking pan that is just the right size to keep the apples close to each other. Put 1 teaspoon of red currant jelly in the cavity of each apple. Pour one tablespoon of cranberry juice over the cavity of each apple. Add a little hot water in the pan (¼ inch). Cover the pan with aluminum foil and bake for 20 minutes. Remove cover and baste with the liquid in the pan. Continue baking uncovered for 4 to 5 minutes. If necessary, add a little more water to avoid burning.

Place each apple in a serving dish. Scrape particles from the pan and transfer the liquid to a saucepan. Blend the liquid with the remaining red currant jelly and bring to a boil over high heat. Pour over the apples, sprinkle with the walnuts, cranberries, and serve immediately.

Acai and Almond Milk Popsicle

serves 4

✓ *Option: You may substitute almond milk with low-fat cow's milk, rice or soy milk.*

ingredients

3½ ounces pure acai, no sugar added (Sambazon smoothie pack)
4 ounces berries (about 1 cup)
1 small banana (about 4 ounces)
4 ounces almond milk

cooking instructions

Place all the fruits and almond milk in a blender. Puree on high speed. Divide equally among 4 popsicle molds and freeze.

Apple and Pear Minestrone

serves 2

ingredients

½ teaspoon grapeseed oil
1 medium apple, diced
(about 5 ounces)
1 medium pear, diced
(about 5 ounces)
1½ teaspoons honey
(or agave nectar)

½ teaspoon pumpkin pie spice
1 inch ginger root, minced
½ teaspoon lemon zest
¾ cup jasmine green tea
(or your favorite)

cooking instructions

Heat the oil in a deep saucepan over high heat. Add the apple and sauté for 2 minutes. Add the pear, pumpkin pie spice, ginger, and zest, then sauté another 1 minute. Add the green tea and bring to boil. Remove from heat and transfer to a serving bowl. Cool to room temperature. Refrigerate for an hour or, for best results, overnight to allow flavors to develop. Serve cold.

Baked Apples with Pomegranate Preserves

✓ *Option: Substitute pomegranate preserves with currant or raspberry preserves.*

serves 4
1 serving: 1 apple

ingredients

4 teaspoons walnuts
4 large apples
9 teaspoons pomegranate preserves
4 tablespoons pomegranate juice
4 tablespoons pomegranate seeds

cooking instructions

Preheat the broiler. Cover the bottom of a baking sheet with parchment paper. Add the walnuts and broil until slightly browned. Remove from the sheet, cool, and chop.

Preheat the oven to 400°F.

Wash and core the apples, being careful not to break through the bottom of the apples. Place them in a baking pan that is just the right size to keep the apples close to each other. Put 1 teaspoon of pomegranate preserves in the cavity of each apple. Pour 1 tablespoon of pomegranate juice into the cavity of each apple. Add a little hot water to the pan (about ¼ inch high). Cover the pan with aluminum foil and bake for 20 minutes. Remove foil and baste with the pan liquids. Continue baking uncovered for 4 to 5 minutes. If necessary, add a little more water to avoid burning.

Place each apple in a serving dish. Scrape particles from the pan and transfer the liquid to a saucepan. Blend the liquid with the remaining pomegranate preserves and bring to boil over high heat. Pour over the apples, sprinkle the walnuts, pomegranate seeds, and serve immediately.

Dates with Almonds

serves 4

✓ *You may also store each portion in a plastic bag for a healthy prepared snack.*

ingredients

8 dates
4 tablespoons almonds

cooking instructions

Divide the dates and almonds in 4 dessert plates and serve immediately.

Pomegranate and Strawberry Parfait

serves 2

ingredients

1½ cups strawberries
2 ounces pure acai, no sugar added
1 teaspoon vanilla extract
1 cup low-fat Greek yogurt
2 tablespoons pomegranate seeds

cooking instructions

Mix the strawberries with vanilla extract and acai. Marinade for 30 minutes. Spoon half the fruit mixture into four parfait glasses. Top with yogurt and finish with the berries. Sprinkle with the pomegranate seeds and serve immediately.

Thin Apple Tart

serves 8

ingredients

2 ounces Old Fashioned
Quaker® Oats
3 ounces whole purpose flour
½ teaspoon cinnamon
Pinch of salt
3 tablespoons grapeseed oil
1 tablespoon vanilla

2 to 3 tablespoons water
2 large apples (about 12 ounces)
2 tablespoons apricot preserves

cooking instructions

Preheat the oven to 475°F.

In a blender, break down the oats to a flour consistency. Place the flours in a bowl. Add the cinnamon, salt, oil, and vanilla, and mix until crumbly. Add 1 tablespoon water and mix into dough. Continue adding water, 1 tablespoon at a time until the dough is smooth and sticks together as one ball. Lay the dough on a wax paper and push down with your palm to flatten a bit. Roll out the dough to a round thin form. Place the dough to a cookie sheet. Brush 1 tablespoon apricot preserves all over the pie dough surface.

Peel and cut in half the apples. Core, quarter, and thinly slice the apples. Starting at the edge of the dough and working inward toward the center, arrange the apple slices in overlapping circles. Finish with another circle of apple slices in the center. Bake for 15 to 20 minutes until golden brown with slightly darker edges. Heat the remaining 1 tablespoon preserves with a little water to thin out in the microwave. Remove the tart from the oven and brush with the preserves. Transfer the tart to a cooling rack.

Winter Fruit Salad

serves 4

ingredients

1 small banana, sliced
1 pear, diced
1 apple, diced
6 ounces grapes
1 orange, peeled and segmented
¼ cup pomegranate seeds
2 tablespoons lemon juice

cooking instructions

Blend all the fruits in a large bowl. Mix in the lemon juice, pomegranate seeds, and refrigerate until use.

Melon Soup

serves 4

ingredients

2 cantaloupes (about 4 cups flesh)
2 tablespoons honey (quickly warmed in the microwave)
4 mint leaves
1 lemon, juiced

cooking instructions

Cut the cantaloupes in half. Remove all the seeds. Spoon out the flesh and place in a blender. Add the honey, mint, and lemon juice. Puree and refrigerate. Serve cold.

References

Fibromyalgia Diet
www.fibromyalgiahealthydiet.com

Fibromyalgia Diet Network
www.fibromyalgiadiet.net

Fibromyalgia Network
www.fmnetnews.com

National Fibromyalgia Association
www.fmaware.org

National Fibromyalgia Research Association
www.nfra.net

Mayo Clinic
www.mayoclinic.com/health/fibromyalgia